DREAMS OF THE FUTURE
DANIEL and REVELATION

BIBLE GUIDES

The twenty-two volumes

★ already published

BIBLE GUIDES

General Editors: William Barclay and F. F. Bruce

No. 22

DREAMS OF THE FUTURE

DANIEL and REVELATION

by

THOMAS S. KEPLER

*Professor of New Testament Language,
and Literature,
Graduate School of Theology,
Oberlin College, U.S.A.*

Published jointly by

LUTTERWORTH PRESS   ABINGDON PRESS

LONDON   NEW YORK AND NASHVILLE

First published 1963

To
JEAN C. HIESTAND
and
LEONARD A. STIDLEY
Whose Dreams of the Future
Are Being Realized

Printed in Great Britain by
Cox & Wyman Ltd., London, Fakenham and Reading

GENERAL INTRODUCTION

THE AIM of Bible Guides is to present in 22 volumes a total view of the Bible, and to present the purpose, plan and power of the Scriptures.

Bible Guides are free from the technicalities of Biblical scholarship but are soundly based on all the generally accepted conclusions of modern Bible research.

They are written in clear, simple, straightforward English. Each author has worked to a comprehensive editorial pattern so that the 22 volumes form a concise conspectus of the Bible.

THE AIM

The aim of Bible Guides is to offer a "guide" to the main themes of each book (or group of books) rather than a commentary on the text of the book. Through Bible Guides the Bible itself will speak its message, reveal its power and declare its purpose.

Bible Guides is essentially an undertaking for non-theologically equipped readers who want to know what the Bible is about, how its various parts came to be written and what their meaning is to-day. But the preacher, teacher, educator and expositor of all ranges of the Christian Church will find Bible Guides a series of books to buy and study. They combine the modern knowledge of the Bible together with all the evangelical zeal of sound Biblical expression—and all done in a handy readable compass.

EDITORIAL PLAN

In our suggestions to the writers of the various books we were careful to make the distinction between a "commentary" and a "guide". Our experience is that an adequate commentary on a book of the Bible requires adequate space and on the part of the student some equipment in the scholarly lore and technicalities of Biblical research. A "guide", however, can be both selective and compressed and do what it sets out to do—guide the reader in an understanding of the book. That has been, and is, our aim.

As general editors we have had a good deal of experience among the various schools of Biblical interpretation. We are constantly surprised at the amount of common Biblical under-standing which is acceptable to all types of Christian tradition and churchmanship. We hope that our Bible Guides reflect this and that they will be widely used, and welcomed as a contribu-tion to Biblical knowledge and interpretation in the twentieth century.

THE WRITERS

The writers of Bible Guides represent a widely selected area of Biblical scholars, and all of them have co-operated enthusiastically in the editorial plan. They conceive their work to be that of examination, explanation and exposition of the book(s) of the Bible each is writing about. While they have worked loyally to the pattern we suggested they have been completely free in their presentation. Above all, they have remembered the present power and appeal of the Bible, and have tried to present its message and its authority for life to-day. In this sense Bible Guides is, we think, a fresh venture in the popular understanding of the Scriptures, combined as it is with the scholarly skill of our company of writers. We owe our thanks also to our publishers and their editors, Dr. Emory Stevens Bucke of the Abingdon Press of New York and Nashville, and Dr. Cecil Northcott of the Lutterworth Press of London. Their careful management and attention to publishing detail have given these Bible Guides a world-wide constituency.

WILLIAM BARCLAY
F. F. BRUCE

The Biblical quotations in this book are
from the Revised Standard Version of the Bible

CONTENTS

POWER OF THE BOOKS

AUTHOR'S FOREWORD

Dreams of the Future

THE MID-YEARS of the twentieth century are similar to the times in which Daniel and Revelation were written. Daniel and Revelation are "tracts for hard times", in which the people then living were unsure about what the future held.

Daniel was written during the reign of Antiochus IV, about 165 B.C., a tyrant who slaughtered Jews who would not worship the Greek god Zeus; while Revelation was compiled during the latter part of the reign of Domitian, about A.D. 95, a vicious Roman emperor who martyred Christians who would not worship him as a god. Each of these periods, the first for the Jews and the second for the Christians, closely parallel the Nazi régime of Hitler in Germany, when both Christians and Jews who refused to "heil" Hitler were put to death for loyalty to their respective faiths.

The Jews passed through the period of persecution under Antiochus IV and came out victorious, yet they wondered about what the future held for them. The Christians came out as valiant people of faith during the reign of Domitian, but they too pondered what future Roman rulers might do to Christians. Hitler and his Nazi régime went the way of Antiochus IV and Domitian, falling into utter destruction; but we find ourselves to-day facing the threat of communism and a third world war.

We have come through past holocausts of war and destruction, but in our time of "cold war" we are wondering what the future holds for us. Daniel and Revelation have a distinct and dynamic message for our times! They are saying to us as they said to their own times: God is in charge of His world; He knows what he is doing; God can never be defeated. James Russell Lowell has phrased exactly what these books are saying to us:

> Though the cause of evil prosper,
> Yet 'tis truth alone is strong:
> Though her portion be the scaffold,
> And upon the throne be wrong,—
> Yet that scaffold sways the future,
> And behind the dim unknown,
> Standeth God within the shadow,
> Keeping watch above His own.

No books of the Bible portray deeper faith in God during difficult times nor possess higher "dreams of the future" than do Daniel and Revelation: both books proclaim the note that the powers of evil can never defeat God's purpose for His righteous followers. They offer a challenge to men and women to-day, or at any time, to stand faithfully with God, when the powers of evil seem regnant; and they show that God has an uncanny way of changing an apparent defeat into a real victory for those who are faithful to Him.

Unfortunately Daniel and Revelation have occasionally been interpreted in the wrong way by the wrong interpreters: namely, as books which make longtime predictions about minute details in history. Rather they are portraits of victorious living in disastrous times to encourage people in future eras to remain steadfast and loyal to God. Daniel and Revelation are not prophetic books to foretell far-distant future events; rather they are *apocalyptic* writings which re-interpret the past so that people in the present will remain faithful and courageous. Like prophetic books, Daniel and Revelation are concerned with the general state of life in the immediate future; but they do not give time tables or detailed charts about particular events centuries beyond the time in which they are written.

I hope the readers of this volume will catch the spirit of courage and the note of hope from Daniel and Revelation for their living in the twentieth century. Daniel and Revelation are great books of faith, and all of us need a similar faith to-day, if we are to share the privilege with God of bringing His Kingdom into history.

THOMAS S. KEPLER

INTRODUCTION

THE NATURE OF APOCALYPTIC WRITINGS

EVERY THOUGHTFUL person and every great world religion is concerned with the question: What will be the final outcome of life upon this planet? We live upon a planet four billion years old, placed in an expanding universe of fifteen billion years of age. *How* all this creation began we do not know; only God knows this great secret. But the person of religious faith believes in a God who in His providence is sharing His creation with us. Since God began life upon this planet, and is in charge of His universe, what will be the final purpose for life on the planet? Apocalyptic writings like Daniel and Revelation have their own definite answers.

Apocalyptic writings find their setting in a concern with the "last things" or "the last events in history," when the world as it is, with all its hopes and dreams, its struggles and sorrows, its joys and accomplishments will finally reach the goal which God intends for His people. At that time rewards will come for the faithful followers of God; His Kingdom will finally have reached its goal on earth. When Jesus proclaimed in His first public utterance, "The time is fulfilled, and the kingdom of God is at hand" (Mark 1: 15), He was speaking about the hope with which all studies of the "last things" are concerned, the Kingdom of God.

The Coming of God's Kingdom

Daniel and Revelation belong to the type of religious literature known as *apocalyptic*. Of all the apocalyptic writings these two stand out as the most interesting, the most meaningful, and the most colorful. An apocalypse is a revelation of God. But an apocalyptic writing has certain particular features which set it apart from other kinds of revelation from God. In the Old Testament we find both *prophetic* and *apocalyptic* writings, each with its "dreams of the future", yet each in a different way holding its religious-theological pattern by which this dream is to be accomplished. Prophetic writings with their hope for the future played their greatest role in the times before the Babylonian exile (before 597 B.C.). The prophets looked upon history as the place where God in His closeness to men would help them bring about His Kingdom on earth. Prophetic thought held a belief that men through struggle and co-operation with God could slowly overcome the evil forces on earth. This would be accomplished through a leader of the line of David, an ideal king who would give leadership to God's chosen people.

This new age, God's Kingdom, might be slow in arriving, and at times it would have reversals, but it would eventually and gradually arrive, for God was One who never could be defeated in His earthly plan. Prophetic thought held to a social gospel, which encouraged faithful persons to work for moral righteousness and social justice. Amos with his cry, "Let justice roll down like waters, and righteousness like an everflowing stream" (Amos 5 : 24), sounded a clarion call for the note of prophecy with its stress on social righteousness. Jeremiah with his hope for the Jews in their homeland after the Babylonian exile, Ezekiel with his dream of the new age after the Babylonian captivity, and Isaiah with his stress on the ideal leader as one who would possess "the spirit of knowledge and the fear of the Lord" (Isaiah 11 : 2) are poignant illustrations of the prophetic concern for "the last things".

After the Babylonian exile (after 538 B.C.) hopes for the new age coming in the prophetic fashion began to be a lost dream, yet a hope that might occur if God would intervene "from above" through a heavenly sent messenger. This present world was too much in the hands of demonic forces to be conquered by any earthly leader; the present world was doomed and could not be improved. In fact, life upon this planet would get worse and worse, until some awful calamity would occur which would invite God's interference into the world with a violent end of things. Then would come the judgment day, when God's faithful servants would inherit the resurrected life, while evil persons would receive their punishment. This pattern of the "last things" which was developed after the exile is known as *apocalyptic*. Sometimes this kind of thought discerned an evil power, such as Satan or the devil, contending with God for allegiances of men and women; and believed that Satan or the devil had his personal demons at work in the world, trying to defeat God and His angels and archangels. Both *prophetic* and *apocalyptic* thought held "dreams of the future", when God and His faithful followers would win, but in different ways.

Just how apocalyptic ideas wove their way into Jewish religious thought is not clear. Some believe they developed of themselves out of harassing times in Jewish life. Others hold that Zoroastrianism from Persia left its apocalyptic influence on Jewish life, since Persia was the world power, 538–332 B.C. In the apocalyptic thought of Zoroastrianism one finds a wise and good personal God Ahura Mazda contending with Angra Mainyu, the power of darkness and evil. Ahura Mazda has his angels to help him, while Angra Mainyu has his demons to aid his cause. In Zoroastrianism one has the story of mankind covering a period of 12,000 years. During the last 1000 years will come the arrival of the saviour Soshyant, through whom Ahura Mazda will bring about the 57 year judgment day, when all mankind will be resurrected from their graves, the faithful followers of Ahura Mazda to receive their rewards, and the followers of Angra Mainyu to receive their punishments. Such ideas show a similarity to the ideas of Daniel and Revelation, when one makes a careful comparison of these writings.

What is Prophetic and Apocalyptic?

The following table summarizes the main differences between *prophetic* and *apocalyptic* "dreams of the future":

Prophetic	*Apocalyptic*
1. Theistic: God is transcendent, "out where the morning stars sing together": but He is immanent, as close as the breath we breathe.	1. Deistic: God is distant from men, ruling this planet from His heavenly abode. He is personal, but not close and immanent as the breath we breathe.
2. God is limited by the free will given to men, but not by Satan or the devil.	2. God is limited by a personal power of evil, known as Satan or the devil.
3. God finds His communion directly with men, not through angels; His Spirit is found within the "heart" of each believer; He has written a "new covenant" in our hearts (Jeremiah 31:31ff.).	3. God is known to men through His angels as Satan is allied with men through demons. God's archangels as special protectors watch over and communicate wisdom to the faithful.
4. There is a hopefulness or betterment for God's Kingdom coming into the present world by means of a social gospel, for social and spiritual progress is possible in the present world. While at times social progress may slip backward, there is a gradual evolution toward the coming of God's Kingdom on earth.	4. A pessimism pervades hope for bettering the present world with a social gospel, for the demonic powers are too strongly woven into the world; social and religious progress is not possible. Conditions will get worse, but after a world-destroying battle, with God's intervention, there will be "a new heaven and a new earth" for the righteous.

Prophetic	Apocalyptic
5. A Messiah (anointed leader) of the line of David, equipped with God's Spirit, will lead mankind into an ultimate time of peace. The Messiah, born among his people, will be their deliverer. The new age lies this side of the grave, "on earth".	5. A Messiah, often known as the "Son of Man," will come from his heavenly place; and upon coming to earth will bring about the defeat of evil on earth with the resurrection day meting out rewards to the faithful, and punishment to the sinful.

Apocalyptic writings are composed with a great amount of fascination. Usually in prose and seldom using poetry, they resort to the use of allegory, myths, numbers and numerology (studies based on number-schemes) and colorful figures of speech to carry their message. Out of the 357 verses in Daniel, but eighteen are in poetry; of the 394 verses in Revelation, only 37 use poetry. The beast of the Roman emperor cult in Revelation is portrayed with ten horns and seven heads; the picture of history in Daniel is depicted in the form of a man, whose head is gold, shoulders are silver, thighs are brass, and feet are iron and clay. Three and one-half years, called "time, times, and half a time," is a real period of suffering in the era of Daniel (168–165 B.C.), when Zeus has replaced Yahweh on the altar in the Jerusalem Temple; but this period of time in Revelation comes to represent a period of awful horror and martyrdom. The number seven is used 54 times in Revelation to depict such objects as churches written to, seals, heads, trumpets, bowls, plagues, while in Daniel a period of seventy years is unravelled as seventy "weeks of years", or seventy times seven. Daniel caricatures the kingdoms of Babylonia, Media, Persia, and Greece as four beasts: a lion with eagle's wings, a bear, a leopard with four wings, and a strong beast with iron teeth and ten horns. God's faithfulness to His chosen people is depicted in Daniel through stories of the three young men unharmed in the fiery furnace and Daniel unmolested in the lions' den. In Revelation the throne is surrounded by a lion, an ox, a man, and an eagle, thus representing all types of humanity; a woman who gives birth to a child is clothed with the sun, the moon under her feet, and a crown of twelve stars upon her head. All of these ways of literary description make books like Revelation and Daniel colorful and mysterious, leaving to the reader the task of unravelling what such expressions mean.

Both Daniel and Revelation, in true fashion of apocalypses, do not give anything definite about their authors. One is by *Daniel*, though the name is not mentioned as the author in the book, and the other is by *John*; but beyond the mere mention of their names the characteristics of the authors are left for the reader to infer. An apocalypse is usually written under someone else's name, attributed to some well-known person of the past, such as Moses, Enoch, Isaiah, or Ezra. The use of a great name from the past gives the book prestige, and lends a more unique authority than to mention the name of the writer himself, a person known by his contemporaries. Just what "John" is the author of Revelation is an enigma; and the "Daniel" in whose name Daniel is written may refer to a "Danel" mentioned in a Danel legend in which God intervened on behalf of the righteous with victory for those who retained their loyalty to the Jewish law; or the name may have been borrowed from a Daniel who is mentioned by Ezekiel with two other heroes, Noah and Job, righteous men of power to deliver (Ezekiel 14: 14), and who is a man of great wisdom (Ezekiel 28: 3).

Authors of an apocalypse sometimes borrow greatly from past religious writings, focusing the materials as their own to meet an impending situation. This is not plagiarism (illegal borrowing) for a writer of an apocalypse, but merely a literary device. While Daniel borrows almost none from earlier writings (only three times from Ezekiel, 17: 23, 31: 6, 28: 2), Revelation borrows

245 times from the Old Testament writings (mainly from Isaiah, Daniel, Ezekiel, Psalms, Exodus, Jeremiah, and Zechariah), once from the Apocrypha, and nine times from the New Testament, along with many references to the Apocrypha and the Pseudepigrapha (see below).

Authentic Apocalypse

Complete apocalyptic writings are few in our Scriptures. Daniel is the only apocalypse in the Old Testament, though there are apocalyptic parts in Isaiah 13–14 and 24–27, Ezekiel 1 and 28–39, Joel 2–3, and Zechariah 9–14. The Apocrypha has but one apocalypse, 2 Esdras, sometimes called The Apocalypse of Ezra—a book with more than one apocalypse in it. The Pseudepigrapha, Jewish writings not allowed in the educational work in the synagogues, contains numerous apocalypses, most important of which is Enoch, which influenced the thought setting in which the New Testament writings were composed. Revelation is the only apocalypse in the New Testament, though some of Paul's writings, especially 1 and 2 Thesssalonians, show a deep impress of apocalyptic thought; and the gospels of Matthew, Mark, and Luke show a vivid influence of apocalyptic ideas. For example, Mark 13 is called "the little apocalypse" and lays the basis for the apocalyptic chapters in Matthew 24 and Luke 21. Yet of all apocalyptic writings Daniel and Revelation stand out as the most beautifully designed in a literary way, as well as the most deeply religiously discerning in their "dreams of the future".

Christian thinking through the last nineteen hundred years has been greatly influenced by apocalyptic thought, particularly by Revelation. Jewish life, on the contrary, especially after the destruction of the Temple in A.D. 70, lost its "dreams of the future" as portrayed in apocalyptic writings, and by the third century of the Christian era Jewish rabbis considered apocalypses as heresies.

THE BOOK OF DANIEL

I. THE HISTORICAL SETTING

THE DETAILS of history cover a period of about 450 years, from the reign of Nebuchadrezzar, when the Babylonian Empire at the battle of Carchemish in 605 B.C. became the world power, to the time when the Maccabeans recaptured the Temple in 165 B.C. and replaced the worship of Zeus by the worship of Yahweh. The following historical chart (most of it found in 1 Maccabees 1: 1-9: 18 and 2 Maccabees 3: 1-7: 42, 8: 1-15: 36) will aid the reader to follow the descriptive background of Daniel, as well as to help him interpret the events:

B.C.

605 Nebuchadrezzar and the Babylonians conquer the Egyptians at Carchemish

605-562 Nebuchadrezzar is king of Babylonia

597 Nebuchadrezzar takes Jerusalem; Jehoiachin with many Jews and the Temple vessels are taken into Babylonian exile

587-586 Fall of Jerusalem; Temple is destroyed; Zedekiah and a second group of Jews are led into Babylonian captivity

556-539 Nabonidus is king of Babylonia, his son Belshazzar, the crown prince, acting as governor for his father in Jerusalem

550 Cyrus of Anshan conquers the Persian Empire

539 Cyrus defeats Nabonidus and conquers Babylonia; he allows Jews to return under Zerubbabel from Babylonian exile

539–530 Cyrus rules over Babylonia as king

530–522 Rule of Cyrus' son Cambyses

522–521 Gaumata tries to usurp the throne in Persia

521–486 Rule of Darius I

520–516 Temple rebuilt under Zerubbabel

486–465 Rule of Xerxes

465–423 Rule of Artaxerxes I

458 Jews return to Jerusalem under Ezra

333 Alexander the Great overthrows the Persian Empire

332 Alexander the Great conquers Palestine

323 Death of Alexander the Great, with his empire divided among his four generals: Cassander rules the west, Macedonia and Greece; Lysimachus rules in the north, Asia Minor as far as Pontus and Paphlagonia; Seleucus rules in the east, Asia as far as the Indus, less Asia Minor; and Ptolemy rules in the south, Egypt with Phoenicia and Coele-Syria. Of these generals the regions governed by Seleucus and Ptolemy form dynasties, battle for possession of Coele-Syria which includes Palestine, and form a background for the book of Daniel:

Seleucids		*Ptolemies*	
312–281	Seleucus I (Nicator)	322–285	Ptolemy I (Soter)
281–261	Antiochus I (Soter)	285–246	Ptolemy II (Philadelphus)
261–246	Antiochus II (Theos)	246–222	Ptolemy III (Euergetes)
246–227	Seleucus II (Callinicus)	222–203	Ptolemy IV (Philopator)
227–223	Seleucus III (Ceraunus)	203–181	Ptolemy V (Epiphanes)

301 Struggle between Ptolemy I and Antigonus for rule of Palestine

250 Antiochus II weds Berenice, daughter of Ptolemy II

223–187 Antiochus III (the Great)

217 Defeat of Antiochus III at Raphia, with loss of territory in Palestine

202 Palestine is reconquered by Antiochus III

198 Antiochus III at the battle of Paneas stops Egypt's hope of retaking Palestine; Antiochus III now invades Phoenicia and takes Gaza

194 Marriage of Cleopatra, daughter of Antiochus III, to Ptolemy V

187 Antiochus III killed at Elymais in Luristan

187–175 Seleucus IV rules

176 Heliodorus tries to plunder the Temple treasuries in Jerusalem

176 Demetrius, elder son of Seleucus IV and rightful inheritor of the throne, is hostage in Rome

175–164 Antiochus IV (Epiphanes) rules

175 Antiochus IV appoints Jason as high priest, deposing Onias III

171 Menelaus replaces Jason as high priest; Onias III is assassinated

170 Ptolemy VI is captured as Antiochus IV invades Egypt; Jason regains office of high priest in Jerusalem, but is deposed by Antiochus IV, who plunders the Temple

169–168 Again Antiochus IV invades Egypt, but is forced by the Romans to evacuate

168 Apollonius conquers Jerusalem, placing troops on the Citadel; the Jewish religion is suppressed by the decree of Antiochus IV

167 The revolt of the Maccabees starts

166–165 Judas Maccabeus leads the Maccabees to victories

165 The Temple is recaptured, recleansed, and rededicated to Jewish worship

164 Death of Antiochus IV at Tabae in Persia

Alexander the Great was fortunate to have Aristotle, the genius of Greek philosophy, as his tutor. Brilliant both by nature and training, Alexander became a general at eighteen and a king at twenty. At the beginning of the fourth century B.C. Greek culture had not too successfully moved into the east. The conquests of Alexander the Great, however, were followed by a movement known as Hellenization (that is, a movement to put Greek thought and customs into life). Certainly there was no better way to unify an empire and at the same time to give its people a high culture. After Alexander had won loyalty in Macedonia and Greece, he crossed the Hellespont in 334 B.C. to challenge Persia, becoming victorious at the River Granicus; defeating the Persians under Darius at Issus; and turning to the south subduing Syria, Palestine, and Egypt; and giving the fatal blow at Gaugamela where he crushed the Persian forces under Darius, and thus became ruler of the Persian Empire. By 327 B.C. his rule extended to western India.

The Upsurge of Greek Life

With his conquests of the nations, Alexander's desire was to Hellenize the Orient. Wherever he won victories he had centers of Greek life initiated. After his death the Ptolemies in Egypt and the Seleucids in Syria carried on his program of instilling the Greek spirit in life. Before many years Alexandria in Egypt vied with Athens as the great center of learning. Ptolemy I had a library and a gymnasium erected here; a Greek translation of the Jewish scriptures was made, known as the Septuagint; toward the beginning of the Christian era a Jewish scholar named Philo wove Greek and Jewish thought together. At Antioch, the main city of Syria, Seleucus I started a school of Greek learning.

Many of the Jews, especially those of the upper classes, welcomed with open arms the introduction of Greek thought, games, and institutions, for it opened to them a new sense of advanced culture; thus they became supporters of assimilation of Jewish and Greek life. Greek names were given to their children; Greek fashions invaded their dress; Greek became the language which paralleled their daily use of Aramaic. Other Jews, however, mainly those who came from a lower social class, resisted the Hellenization of life, partly because they were unable to understand Greek ideas and partly because they had been citizens whose abode was mainly Palestine, with no contact with the wider world of the empire. But there were deeper causes for resisting Hellenization for both the humble and the highly trained Jews: namely, reasons of a nationalistic and a religious nature. The wealthy and the aristocratic joined the poor and the humble in forming themselves into the Hasidim, a "holy people" who vowed not to allow Greek life to infect their Jewish way of existence. Out of such a group arose the party known as the Pharisees ("separatists"), who believed that the best way to combat Hellenization was by "separating" themselves from its mode of living, and by being deeply loyal to the ways of Jewish culture.

Antiochus III was a strong advocate of Hellenization. In 198 B.C., after he had been victorious in the battle of Paneas, he found a number of assimilationist Jews awaiting him with enthusiasm as he returned to Jerusalem. In Jerusalem at that time were two main families, the Oniads and the Tobiads. The Tobiads held the chief financial seat and were loyal to the Seleucids, while the Oniads controlled the high priest's office and held allegiance to the Ptolemies. With favoritism of many shown toward Antiochus III, the gap between the two rival families in Jerusalem was greatly widened. Had Hellenization been merely an attempt to invade Jewish life, the outcome might have been peaceful. But as it became confused with both political and religious problems, embodying the chief families of Jerusalem, dire trouble could be expected.

After Antiochus IV came to power the Hellenizing party at Jerusalem sought permission to build a Greek gymnasium in Jerusalem. Meanwhile, when Onias III the high priest was away from Jerusalem, Jason his brother, a pro-Seleucid, offered money to Antiochus IV for the office of high priest. Antiochus IV gave him the office, which to him seemed all right, since Jason was of the Oniad high priest family; but the Jewish Hasidim did not see it so, retaining their loyalty to Onias. Jason desired the assimilation of Jewish life to Hellenistic culture: he sent a silver offering to the god Hercules at Tyre, along with representatives to the games in honor of this deity. After Jason had been high priest for less than three years, Menelaus (not an Oniad) paid Antiochus IV more money for the office of high priest, thus causing Jason to flee, and instigating the assassination of Onias III. Menelaus with his brother Lysimachus stole and sold vessels from the Temple to pay for the office of high priest. Riots ensued; and Jason, knowing of the absence of Antiochus IV in Egypt, re-captured the office of high priest from Menelaus, only to have Antiochus IV return, reappoint Menelaus as high priest, punish the Jews for resisting Menelaus, and plunder the Temple. The Jewish people refused to accept Menelaus as high priest, thus inviting the persecutions of Antiochus IV, who brought back his army from Egypt to slaughter the Jewish loyalists and to rob the Temple, taking such articles as the golden candlestick and the sacred table.

The Altar to Zeus

Two years later the city walls were razed, and a garrison of Syrian soldiers was placed in the fortified city of Akra, the old City of David. Antiochus IV forbade sabbath observances, the

Temple services, the rite of circumcision, and food laws; he destroyed the sacred books and parts of the Temple, and on 15 Kislev (December 25, 168 B.C.) he set up an altar to the god Zeus, forcing Jews to sacrifice swine to this Greek deity. Altars to Zeus were built throughout Palestine, where Jews were forced to offer swine as sacrifices. At one of these altars in a small town called Modein, a local priest Mattathias refused to sacrifice offerings to Zeus, and in a fit of anger killed a renegade Jewish priest who was offering swine, slew an officer of the king, and destroyed the altar to Zeus. Mattathias and his five sons fled to the hills, organized the Jewish red-blooded sympathizers, and destroyed altars to Zeus about the country.

After Mattathias's death in 166 B.C. the reins of leadership fell into the hands of Judas, whom they called "the Hammerer", or "Maccabeus". Judas led the Jewish revolters in guerilla warfare, with victories at Beth-horon, Emmaus, and Bethsura. When the Syrian leaders withdrew to Antioch to prepare greater forces for combat, Judas and his men attacked Jerusalem, capturing the city except the Citadel. The Temple was cleansed of pagan objects, the altar to Yahweh was rebuilt, and sacrifices were again made to Yahweh on December 25, 165 B.C., just three years after the Temple had been desecrated in honor of Zeus. Loyal Jews in Gilead, Idumaea, and Galilee were rescued by Judas's forces, and peace was made with the Syrian general Lysias, who allowed religious freedom to the Jews. In 164 B.C. Antiochus IV fell ill and died at Tabae in Persia. Having secured religious freedom, the Jewish people wanted also political freedom, and in fighting for this Judas Maccabeus was killed in 160 B.C., his army being destroyed at Elasa.

Judas Maccabeus and his forces had thus won religious freedom for the Jews, but not political freedom. An alliance was made with the Romans in 161 B.C. for the purpose of securing this political freedom, but it was of little benefit for the Jews.

The Romans kept their hands off Palestine until they took over in 63 B.C. For a short time after 142 B.C., in the days of Simon, the Jews enjoyed political freedom, when "the yoke of the Gentiles was removed from Israel, and the people began to write in their documents and contracts" (1 Maccabees 13: 41, 42). But this was only momentarily. After 63 B.C., when Pompey the Roman general controlled Palestine for the Romans, political freedom disappeared.

The rebellion led by Judas Maccabeus had thus been successful in bringing religious freedom to the Jews, but the question began to arise: What lay ahead for the loyal Jews in the future? Could the Jews stand out against the royal forces of Antiochus IV? Would there by any hope for the Jews in time to come? Out of such querying and fear came the triumphant answer in the book of Daniel, calling the Jewish people to heroic faith in God. By relating stories of Daniel and his three friends (Shadrach, Meshach, and Abednego) the author illustrates how God had saved faithful followers in the past from terrors like the fiery furnace and a lions' den: and He would do the same in the days that lay ahead. By relating stories about Nebuchadrezzar, Belshazzar, and Darius the author infers that earthly kings are no match for God as the omnipotent King, whose plan for history can never be overthrown by earthly potentates. God has a secret plan for the destiny of history, which Daniel the seer is able to unravel. Daniel, like Revelation, is a book meant for hard times to show that God can never be defeated. It is a writing to encourage people to be faithful unto death itself, for only the faithful are allied to God's Kingdom which can never be destroyed!

2. DANIEL WRITES HIS APOCALYPSE

A STUDY of the book of Daniel entails five introductory questions, after the historical background of the book is known:

(1) *Who* wrote the book? (2) *When* was it written? (3) *Why* was it written? (4) *What plan* did the writer have in composing his book? (5) *What mode of interpretation* can we employ to understand the book? Naturally the answers to these questions overlap. When these questions have been answered, then the exposition of the book naturally becomes simplified. The student of the Bible has two ways to satisfy these five queries: one by studying the internal text of the book, and the other by knowing the external historical conditions surrounding the composition of the book. With these two factors in mind, let us first look carefully at the author and the date of Daniel.

The Author and the Date

The book of Daniel covers Old Testament history from the time of Nebuchadrezzar (605–562 B.C.) until the period of Antiochus IV (175–164 B.C.). Upon first glance at the book it appears that its author is living during the time of Nebuchadrezzar and is predicting events from then to 165 B.C., when the Temple was recaptured by the Maccabees from the Syrians. Though Daniel is never named as its author, many have assumed that the author is a Daniel, who lived during the reign of Nebuchadrezzar. The name Daniel means "God has given decision". There is a man of great faith, wisdom, and "decision" mentioned as Daniel by Ezekiel, which has made some assume this Daniel as the author. Of this Daniel we find Ezekiel writing that in a land which sins against God "even if these three men, Noah, Daniel, and Job, were in it, they would deliver but their own lives by their righteousness" (14: 14; also 14: 20); and that the Lord speaks to the prince of Tyre: "You are indeed wiser than Daniel" (28: 3). The Ras Shamra text also indicates that there was a Danel (Daniel), about whom there was a Jewish legend during the time of the Babylonian captivity (597–538 B.C.), whose righteousness invited divine interference which brought about reward and triumph for the Jews who remained loyal to the Jewish law.

There are, however, a number of factors which make it difficult for this Daniel living at the time of Nebuchadrezzar to be the author of Daniel: (1) About 200 B.C. the *Prophets* were added to the *Law* to compose the Jewish "Bible". Yet Daniel is not among the *Prophets*, being added to the *Sacred Writings* about A.D. 90, when the Jewish "Bible" was completed. (2) The book of Daniel is not mentioned in any Jewish literature until 140 B.C., when the Sibylline Oracles (3 : 397–400) refer to it. In Baruch 1 : 15–3 : 3 (written about 150 B.C.) there is a prayer similar to that in Daniel 9: 4ff. The book of Daniel is also alluded to in 1 Maccabees 2 : 59ff. (written about 125 B.C.). Daniel is referred to 164 times in 1 Maccabees, the Sibylline Oracles, and Enoch (written about 95 B.C.). (3) Jesus ben Sirach, about 190 B.C., lists the great men of Jewish history (Ecclesiasticus 44 : 1–50 : 24); but among these names that of Daniel is missing. (4) Words borrowed from the Babylonian, Persian, and Greek languages appear in Daniel. (5) Jeremiah is mentioned as a prophet (9: 2) and his writings are referred to. (6) In Jeremiah's time (also the period of Nebuchadrezzar) the Chaldeans are spoken of as a nation or people, referring to the Babylonians; but in the book of Daniel they are known as astrologers, magicians, diviners of truth. (7) The book of Daniel was written partly in Aramaic, a language popular among the Jews in the second century B.C., but not at the time of Nebuchadrezzar. (8) The author has an excellent view of history after the time of Alexander the Great, especially during the Maccabean struggles; but his history shows many inaccuracies during the Babylonian and Persian periods. (9) The theology regarding the resurrection of the dead and ideas about angels show that the author lived at a later time than that of Nebuchadrezzar. The same may be said in regard to his concern for diet, fasting, and ritualistic prayers. (10) The pattern and purpose of the book of Daniel as an apocalypse, which *reinterprets* history from the time of Nebuchadrezzar until the time of Judas Maccabeus and Antiochus IV, and written in 165 B.C., fits better into the scheme and purpose of Daniel than if the book were written in the period of Nebuchadrezzar, predicting history for the next 450 years.

Who the writer of Daniel is we cannot know, for in true apocalyptic custom he does not make his name known. But we can infer certain qualities about the author: (1) He is a man of great faith, possibly a Hasid, who in his "dreams of the future" is certain that God's plan for history will in the end be victorious. (2) He is a literary artist, skilled in his use of figures of speech, numbers, myths, and colorful stories to clothe his book into one of the most fascinating apocalypses ever written. (3) He is a scholarly person well versed in Greek history, seemingly "at home" amidst a variety of historical facts and events to make the message of his book both historically sound, as well as religiously deep. A scholar more of his own times, he lacks historical accuracy when discussing the Persian and Babylonian periods. (4) He is a skilled allegorist. As John Bunyan in his *Pilgrim's Progress* emerges as the greatest allegorist of the English language, the author of Daniel shows himself as the most colorful allegorist of the Old Testament writers. In each chapter of Daniel a spiritual lesson is to be found, but at the same time each figure, person, beast, or number is to be unravelled. (5) He is no "armchair" theorist, but a man who seems a part of the times in which he lives, and one who writes out of a vivid feeling for the tragic situation which comes out of the reign of Antiochus IV. He is an interpreter of history, not a prophet, who writes in 165 B.C. to share his faith, woven out of the hard facts of life, with his fellow countrymen. (6) He uses fictional allegory to secure an audience, for he would have found it difficult to impress people with his message by appearing in person. Prophetic inspiration was thought to have expired about 400 B.C. at the time of Ezra. In true apocalyptic fashion he puts himself and his message as though it were before 400 B.C., not to defraud but to impress people with his message, which he feels is inspired by God to encourage the people of his day.

3. PLAN OF THE BOOK

DANIEL IS a well-planned book, falling into two parts: Part One, which deals with a series of faith-stories about Daniel and his three friends, Shadrach, Meshach, and Abednego (1-6); and Part Two, which imparts in four visions of Daniel an interpretation of world history from the time of Nebuchadrezzar to the reign of Antiochus. The book is a unity—one work— except for the few verses in the last chapter, 12: 5-12, where possibly an editor (or two editors) has attempted to correct Daniel's predictions about the resurrection day being 1290 or 1335 days, instead of 1150 days, after the desecration of the Temple by Antiochus IV on December 25, 168 B.C. The book is written in colorful fashion; it is alluring to read, vital in language, dramatic in illustration. While each story is a religious tale in itself, and coming out of a certain historical period, the stories are tied around a common religious theme: *have faith in the future, as you learn from the past, for God will never forsake those who are faithful to Him.*

There are three Additions to Daniel, included by Jerome in his Latin translation, known as the Vulgate, which are a part of the Apocrypha and are included in the Bible used by the Roman Catholic Church. They are: The Prayer of Azariah and the Hymn of the Three Men, The Story of Susanna, and the Story of

Bel and the Dragon. Azariah is the one whom the chief of eunuchs in the reign of Nebuchadrezzar called Abednego, and his prayer is offered in the setting where the three young men, Shadrach, Meshach, and Abednego, are placed in the fiery furnace. The Hymn of the Three Men, "O All ye Works of the Lord, Bless ye the Lord", is offered by the three in gratitude to God after their deliverance from the flaming furnace. The Story of Susanna shows Daniel's wisdom in absolving a virtuous Jewish maiden from the accusation of adultery by two unscrupulous elders, when Daniel has each of these elders testify individually. The story of Bel and the Dragon is composed of two rather inferior stories to show Daniel's wisdom: Daniel shows that the priests of Bel are the ones who consume the provisions offered daily to Bel. The monstrous dragon worshipped in Babylonia is shown to be an idol, and bursts apart after Daniel feeds it a mixture of pitch, fat, and hair; this leads to Daniel being put into the lions' den, yet he is unharmed because God with the help of the prophet Habakkuk is aiding him. These stories, composed a century later than the book of Daniel, are interesting to read, they carry on the note of wisdom and faithfulness of the man Daniel, but they add nothing novel to the original teaching of the book of Daniel.

The book of Daniel has come into our hands partly in Hebrew and partly in Aramaic, the latter being the popular language understood by the people of the time: 1: 1–2: 4a, 8–12 are in Hebrew; 2: 4b–7: 28 are in Aramaic. Some scholars believe that the whole of the book of Daniel was originally written in Aramaic, so that it could be read and understood by all, the author desiring it to be a popular book; and that parts of it were later translated into the Hebrew, the sacred language, to ensure its reception into the canon of Sacred Writings about A.D. 90 at the Council of Jamnia, when the rabbis closed the Old Testament. Others hold that the author wrote the first part (chapters 1–7) in

35

Aramaic, but later composed the second part (chapters 8–12) in the sacred language of Hebrew; and that when he combined these two sections he translated 1: 1—2: 4a into the Hebrew, possibly being prevented from translating the entire book into Hebrew by death. Though the language in which Daniel may have been originally written is not agreed upon by scholars, there is a unified opinion that it speaks in a tremendous way the "language" or Spirit of God to its own time, as well as to the centuries that followed its composition. That is why at the Council of Jamnia it was canonized as part of the Sacred Scriptures; and that is why it is "canonized" in the hearts of so many people through the centuries and to-day. It is "inspired" scripture, which continues to inspire the hearts of its readers.

An outline of the book of Daniel follows this plan:

(a) *Six Stories of the Faith of Daniel and his Friends*

1. Daniel and his friends by their training show themselves to Nebuchadrezzar as ten times wiser than other seers (1: 1–21).
2. Nebuchadrezzar's dream about the image whose head is of gold, breasts and arms of silver, belly and thighs of bronze, and feet of iron and clay, along with the stone, is unravelled by Daniel, for which he and his three friends are rewarded with political positions in Babylon (2: 1–49).
3. The three friends will not worship the golden image of Nebuchadrezzar, but are unscathed when fed to the fiery furnace, and are then rewarded by Nebuchadrezzar (3: 1–30).
4. Nebuchadrezzar's dream of the tree which reaches to heaven, with his eating of grass with the beasts of the field, is interpreted by Daniel (4: 1–37).
5. At the feast of Belshazzar, where the king profanes the Temple vessels, Daniel foretells the meaning of the handwriting on the wall as relative to the downfall of Belshazzar (5: 1–30).

6. Daniel will not obey the decree to worship king Darius and is placed in the lions' den, where God delivers Daniel from harm (6: 1–28).

(b) Four Visions of Daniel and their Meaning

1. A vision and a dream in the first year of Belshazzar about the four beasts: the lion with eagle's wings, the bear, the leopard with four wings on its back, and the strong beast with iron teeth and ten horns, out of which comes the little horn, is related to history from the time of Nebuchadrezzar to Antiochus IV (7: 1–28).
2. A vision in the third year of Belshazzar about the ram with two horns butting the he-goat whose horn breaks into four parts, out of which comes a little horn; Gabriel informs Daniel that these refer to the Medes and Persians meeting the Greeks under Alexander the Great, whose kingdom is divided among his four generals, from one of which comes Antiochus IV (8: 1–27).
3. In the first year of Darius, Gabriel informs Daniel that the seventy years before the desolations in Jerusalem refer to "weeks of years", or seventy times seven years, which equals 490 years before the abominations (9: 1–27).
4. In the third year of Cyrus, after the vision of a man on the bank of the Tigris, Daniel is informed that Michael will stand by him to bring the resurrection day, on which the martyrs will be rewarded and the awful sinners punished; this will happen after the story of secular history with its victories of rulers, its intrigues of leaders, and its final destruction of Jerusalem occurs; all of this will happen, Daniel is told, 1150 days (or is it 1290 or 1335 days?) after the desecration of the Temple by Antiochus IV on December 25, 168 B.C. (10: 1–12: 13).

In compiling the materials in Daniel the author is using allegory as the literary means on which to tie historical facts. Many of his historical details, especially those from the time of Alexander the Great to Antiochus IV, are accurate, indicating that he is a careful student of Greek history. Other details, as related to the periods of Babylonian and Persian history, are less accurate. But this makes little difference to the author of Daniel, since his main purpose is religious instruction to instill faith rather than historical instruction to educate his listeners about secular facts. Historical stories are but the framework for the religious message of faith which he wants his readers to catch. He is attempting to have his readers place themselves in several historical periods, such as those of Nebuchadrezzar, Cyrus, Belshazzar, Alexander the Great, Darius, in order that they get a feel of those times; and then by allegorizing those times through numbers, dreams, myths, fiery furnaces, lions' dens to have his readers catch a gleam of faith for their own times.

The main thesis in Daniel is: God cannot be defeated, nor will God ever allow His faithful followers to be defeated. Righteousness and faithfulness are finally rewarded by God. To the degree that the readers of Daniel caught this note of faith, to that degree was the author's purpose well accomplished. He is not predicting the events of history from a perspective in Nebuchadrezzar's reign, but is reinterpreting history during the persecutions of Antiochus IV, to show that as God has undergirded and rewarded His faithful followers in the past, He will continue to do so in the present and in the future.

There are some who feel that two authors can be seen at work in the Book of Daniel, since the book is so vividly divided in two parts: (1) chapters 1–6, stories relating to Daniel and his friends; (2) chapters 7–12, the visions of Daniel. Those who hold to the idea of two authors would discern a writer who in the third century B.C. compiled the first part of Daniel, mostly in

Aramaic; while the second section was added at the time of the Maccabean rebellion, about 165 B.C., largely in Hebrew. Yet there seems to be a real unity in the entire book, which points to a single author who perhaps worked the earlier materials together into the Book of Daniel.

4. PURPOSE OF THE BOOK

UNFORTUNATELY the book of Daniel in our English Bible has been placed among the books of prophecy, with Daniel as a major prophet. The Jewish scriptures, as we have seen, placed it among the Sacred Writings, canonized at the Council of Jamnia about A.D. 90. Daniel was put among the prophets because a type of scholarship believed that Daniel lived during the time of Nebuchadrezzar, and that God had given him the uncanny wisdom to unravel both small and large details for 450 years of future history. But Daniel was not this kind of a foreteller, and had he made predictions for such a long span of time, we wonder if he would have had an audience, if his writings would have been saved, and if the book of Daniel would have had a valuable purpose.

Should anyone to-day make minute predictions about events in world history between now and the year A.D. 2400, he would not be likely to have an audience. He would merely be labelled a fanatic. However, when an interpreter of history, such as Arnold Toynbee, gives us a conclusion that out of the story of the past civilizations most cultures destroyed themselves because of a moral breakdown, we listen attentively and say to ourselves: This is a moral universe. Nations, like persons, reap what they sow! And so it was with the author of Daniel. He takes six stories about Daniel and his three friends (Shadrach, Meshach, and Abednego) to show that *a faithful person can never be defeated and destroyed* (1: 1–6: 28), and four visions of Daniel to show in an interpretation of history that *righteousness and faithfulness will ultimately triumph over sin and apostasy* (7: 1–12: 13).

(1) The spiritual training of these four young men convinces Nebuchadrezzar that they are ten times wiser than other seers: *God gives wisdom to those who abide by His laws* (1: 1–20).

(2) God empowers Daniel to foretell the meaning of Nebuchadrezzar's dream about the man whose head is of gold, his breast and arms of silver, his belly and thighs of bronze, and his feet of iron and clay as being the nations of Babylonia, Media-Persia, Greece, and the Ptolemies of Egypt and the Seleucids of Syria; and that the stone which destroys the image of the man is the Kingdom of God. For possessing this wisdom Daniel is given the award, along with the awards for his three friends, of the rule of Babylon and the headship of the wise men of Babylon: *The lesson thus is, Faithfulness is always rewarded by God* (2: 1–49).

(3) Shadrach, Meshach, and Abednego will not worship the golden image of Nebuchadrezzar; and when thrown into the fiery furnace they are unscathed. Nebuchadrezzar withdraws his decree for Jews to worship the image; and then rewards the three young men by giving them promotions in the province of Babylon: *From this story we learn, Nothing can harm righteous persons, for God will care for them and will reward them for their faith* (3: 1–30).

(4) Daniel interprets Nebuchadrezzar's dream of a tree reaching to heaven and visible throughout the earth, which is cut down, and the king eating grass with the beasts of the field, but having his reason restored after he praises God, as having reference to Nebuchadrezzar: *It teaches that no king can vie against the power of God who is the King of kings, and who has the power to destroy and to redeem earthly kings* (4: 1–37).

(5) King Belshazzar drinks at one of his banquets from the vessels of the Temple, thus mocking God, only to discern the

handwriting on the wall. Daniel interprets *Mene, Tekel, Peres* as meaning: "God has numbered the days of your kingdom, and brought it to an end . . . You have been weighed in the balances and found wanting . . . Your kingdom is divided and given to the Medes and the Persians." Daniel is rewarded with gold and purple, and made third ruler of the kingdom. And on that same night Belshazzar is slain! The lesson here is plain: *You cannot mock the God of the universe, you cannot profane the sacred; this is a moral universe and you must treat God with sacredness* (5: 1–30).

(6) When Daniel is put into the lions' den because he will not obey the decree to worship Darius, but instead worships God and is unharmed by the lions, another lesson is discerned: *You cannot harm a faithful person for God will protect him at all times* (6: 1–28).

Daniel's Primary Purpose

The author of Daniel has one primary purpose in telling these "faith stories" of the past about the four righteous young men: If God has protected His faithful followers as they confronted times of danger, mockery, persecution, and martyrdom in the times of Nebuchadrezzar, Darius, and Belshazzar, and has rewarded them for their righteousness, He will continue at all times to do the same for His loyal followers, even during the time of the Maccabean revolt and in the days that follow. Do not worry about the future; live one day at a time faithfully; God will reward you for your steadfast loyalty. God is always the God of history, and as He has given rewards in past centuries to His saintly followers, He will continue to do so to-day and always. Be faithful to God and He will be faithful to you, for the righteous man lives by faith. *Never forsake God and He will never forsake you*, is Daniel's lesson from the past.

In the last six chapters of Daniel (7: 1–12: 13) the author in four dreams of Daniel attempts to clarify the meaning of history, showing how glories in the past were given temporarily to the pagan nations of the world, each in its turn to meet destruction; but that finally the everlasting glories would be given by God to His faithful followers on a resurrection day. The thesis and lesson of each chapter is as follows:

(1) Daniel dreams in the first year of Belshazzar (the crown prince, son of Nabonidus) about four great beasts coming out of the sea: a lion with eagle's wings, a bear with three ribs between its teeth in its mouth, a leopard with four wings on its back, and a terrible and strong beast with iron teeth and ten horns. These four kingdoms represent the Babylonians, the Medes, the Persians, and the Hellenistic kingdoms, with the ten horns signifying the ten kings from Alexander the Great (336–323 B.C.) to the young son of Seleucus IV (187–175 B.C.) who should have succeeded his father in 175. The little horn, "before which three horns were plucked up by their roots," is Antiochus IV (175– 164 B.C.), who is preceded by Seleucus IV, Heliodorus, and Seleucus's young son (who was also called Antiochus). But these kingdoms will not last, for "one like the Son of man", the representative of the kingdom of the saints, will usher in an ever-lasting kingdom for the righteous (7: 1–28). The lesson is: *Pagan nations have their day of glory, soon to be destroyed; but God's Kingdom brings an eternal reward to His saintly followers.*

(2) Daniel's second dream is set in the third year of King Belshazzar at Susa in Elam. Gabriel gives Daniel the wisdom that the ram of two horns represents the Medes and the Persians, and that the he-goat with one horn indicates Alexander the Great. When they meet in 333 B.C. Alexander the Great will defeat the Persian Empire (which absorbs the Medes), only to have his empire divided among his four generals after his death in 323 B.C.: to Cassander, Lysimachus, Seleucus, and Ptolemy. Again the reference to the little horn means Antiochus IV, who will desecrate

the Temple in 168 B.C. But this tragedy will be only temporary, for in 1150 days (nearly three and one-half years) the Temple will be recaptured and the altar will be rededicated to Yahweh (8: 1–27).˙ The teaching of this story is clear: *Earthly powers destroy one another; they are temporal. For a time Zeus will be on the altar, but finally God will be worshipped in His rightful sanctuary. Do not turn traitor worshipping Zeus!* (And all of this occurred on December 25, 165 B.C., when the Temple was recaptured and rededicated.)

(3) The third vision occurs in the first year of Darius's reign, in which Gabriel again tells Daniel the meaning of seventy years mentioned by Jeremiah regarding the end of the desolations in Jerusalem. He interprets Jeremiah's prophecy by discerning seventy years as "weeks of years", that is, seventy times seven, or 490 years; then will come the day of reward for the faithful and the destruction of the one who desecrates the Temple. His chart is as follows: seven weeks of years (49 years)=Zedekiah (586 B.C.) to Joshua the high priest (538 B.C.); sixty-two weeks of years (435 years)=Joshua to the assassination of Onias III the high priest (171 B.C.); one week (seven years)=from Onias's death to the desecration of the Temple, followed by the death of Antiochus IV (164 B.C.), during which time the Temple will be desecrated for half a week, three and one-half years (168–165 B.C.) The lesson from this story is plain: *An interpretation from the predictions of Jeremiah indicates that the end of the one who desecrates the Temple is near at hand. Hold on with faith! The end-time is near!*

(4) The fourth vision has its setting in the third year of Cyrus, king of Persia, when one "in the likeness of the sons of men" (10: 16) touches his lips and gives him this wisdom: Cyrus will be succeeded by Darius I, Xerxes, and Artaxerxes (11: 2); then Alexander the Great will come into his power, and his kingdom will be divided among his four generals after his death (11: 3–4);

an alliance will be made as Berenice, daughter of Ptolemy II, marries Antiochus II; but the wedded couple will be murdered through a plan of Laodice, Antiochus' divorced wife (11: 6); Syria will be invaded and plundered by Ptolemy III to avenge his sister Berenice (11: 7–9); after battles between Seleucus III and Antiochus III, Ptolemy IV will be victorious at Raphia over Antiochus III, though later Antiochus III will capture Palestine from Ptolemy V (11: 10–16); Ptolemy V will marry Antiochus's daughter Cleopatra (11: 17); Antiochus III will be defeated by the Romans in 190 B.C., as he carries his conquests into Greece and Asia Minor, and will be killed in 187 B.C. as he attempts to plunder the temple at Elymais (11: 18–19); Seleucus IV will be assassinated in 175 B.C. as he tries to exact tribute (11: 20); Antiochus IV, not Demetrius the rightful heir, will succeed Seleucus IV (11: 21); he will assassinate Onias III the high priest (11: 22–24), carry a successful campaign into Egypt and ravage Palestine (11: 25–27); and after the Romans hinder another campaign of Antiochus IV into Egypt in 168 B.C., he will return to Jerusalem, where he will put Zeus on the Temple altar, forbid Jewish worship of their God, will have a Syrian garrison brought into Jerusalem (11: 28–31); a great division will ensue between the Hellenizers and the Hasidim in Jerusalem, awful persecutions will occur (11: 32–35); Antiochus IV will assume titles of divinity, local temples will be desecrated (11: 36–39), then Antiochus IV will defeat Ptolemy Philometer, to control Egypt, Libya, and Ethiopia (11: 40–43); Antiochus IV will come to his destruction at a place between Palestine and the Great Sea (11: 44–45)—which is incorrect, since Antiochus IV dies at Tabae in Persia in 164 B.C.

44

The Resurrection Day

When Antiochus IV has died, then the resurrection day will be near at hand, but its occurrence will not be until dire and terrifying calamities take place; but Michael the protector of Israel will watch over the faithful. When the resurrection day arrives, all whose names have been written in the book of life will be delivered. Among the dead who are resurrected, the martyrs will share the reward of everlasting life, while the most sinful persons will share everlasting shame and contempt. The day of the resurrection is but "a time, two times, and half a time" away; that is, but three and one-half years distant; it is at hand (12: 1–4). To reckon the end of the three and one-half years, begin with December 25, 168 B.C., when the Temple was desecrated, and you will work out the resurrection day in 164 B.C.—it is almost here! [Since the resurrection day did not occur in 164 B.C., after 1150 days (three and one-half years), two attempts were made, possibly by editors, to make new predictions: one sights it to occur in 1290 days; another, following the same plan of the Ascension of Isaiah 4: 12, places the resurrection day after 1335 days.] But remain faithful each day; whenever the great day arrives, you will be judged by your faithfulness to God! (10: 1—12: 13). The lesson here is one of new hope in the resurrection from the dead: *If you ally yourself with earthly kingdoms, see how they come and go; notice how temporal they are. God's Kingdom is an eternal kingdom. It is better to be faithful to God's kingdom, even though you suffer as a martyr, than to retain loyalty to an earthly kingdom; for God will give His loyal and faithful followers citizenship in an everlasting kingdom, soon to be initiated by Michael for God's faithful followers.*

What is the purpose of these four visions? They place before the Jewish people of 165 B.C. a proposition: If you turn traitor to Yahweh and do not remain true to Him and to the Temple cult,

45

you will not be punished by Antiochus IV and his Syrian forces; life temporarily will not be harassed by persecution. But it is better to take the long view of life, and to ally yourself with God and the Temple cult of Yahweh; for even though you become a martyr for such a faithfulness, your reward will be one of an everlasting nature; you will on the resurrection day share citizenship in God's Eternal Kingdom. Temporal kingdoms will come and go, but God's Kingdom is everlasting. Earthly kingdoms deal with time; God's Kingdom deals with eternity!

THE BOOK OF REVELATION

RECENTLY AN interesting and vital commentary on Revelation was written entitled *The Last Book of the Bible*, by Hanns Lilje. The author, a German Protestant bishop, wrote this volume while a prisoner in a Gestapo prison camp guarded by Nazi soldiers. In his condition of persecution in time of war, because as a Christian he would not bow down to Adolf Hitler, he found the book of Revelation speaking to his heart. And it should have done this, because the book of Revelation was written by John in a similar circumstance in a concentration camp about A.D. 95 on the Isle of Patmos during the last days of the reign of the Roman emperor Domitian. Christians were being persecuted by Domitian if they would not worship him as a god. The message of Revelation leaped across the changing centuries to the spiritual encouragement of Bishop Hanns Lilje, because it spoke to the unchanging needs of a Christian in times of persecution.

Emperor Worship

It is difficult for modern persons to think of emperors being worshipped as gods, but such a religious custom was not uncommon in the pre-Christian centuries. Egyptian Pharaohs had claimed descent from gods and were worshipped with prayers and hymns; Greek legendary heroes such as Heracles were turned into gods after their deaths; Alexander the Great and those succeeding him received divine homage, with a tyrant like Antiochus

47

IV having coins minted with the inscription "King Antiochus, god manifest"; hence his title Antiochus *Epiphanes*. But in none of the pre-Christian cultures, until the time of the Roman Empire, was the worship of emperors organized into a rigid political-religious system. Julius Caesar, who established his personal dominion over the Roman world, had his statue placed among the gods in the temples, and after his death (44 B.C.) he was declared a god by the Senate. Seventeen years after the assassination of Julius Caesar, Octavius became Roman emperor, and to Octavius was given the title *Augustus*, a title up to this time reserved for the gods. Octavius Augustus forbade the worship of himself as a god, though he allowed temples throughout the provinces to be erected to the goddess *Roma* (the state of Rome). After his death in A.D. 14 the Roman Senate declared him a god, and had a temple built in his honor on the Palatine hill in Rome. Soon he was worshipped throughout the Roman Empire.

With the Roman emperor cult thus widely spread, temples of worship could be found in many of the great centers of the Mediterranean world; but most emperors were content with leaving the worship of themselves by the citizens on a voluntary basis. Emperors like Tiberius (A.D. 14–37) and Claudius (A.D. 41–54) tried to forbid the citizens to pay worship to them, but other emperors were concerned that worship of them be taken seriously by the people. Caligula (A.D. 37–41) demanded universal worship of his statue, which brought great persecutions of the Jews at Alexandria and Jamnia who failed to comply. Towards the end of his reign Caligula ordered a statue of himself to be erected as Zeus Manifest and put in the Jerusalem Temple, with Roman soldiers placed there to see that Jewish worship of him was enforced. However, the spirit of popular opinion and the resistance of the Jews so aroused the friends of Caligula that the order was withdrawn; then Caligula recanted and again insisted that his bust be worshipped in the Jewish Temple. But soon

Caligula was murdered, and the problem of the Jews worshipping Roman emperors ceased.

Vespasian (A.D. 69–79) was another emperor who exalted himself and his family within the emperor cult. He gave his wife the title of *Augusta* (an epithet to a goddess). Though he never declared himself the son of a god, he felt that he was the heir of Augustus's politics. Peace, Victory, and Fortune were three political words which he greatly emphasized. He was called Benefactor and Savior by his people. Elaborate services of worship and ceremony were offered in his behalf. Some scholars have felt that Revelation might have been written during the reign of Vespasian, since his reign follows almost immediately after the reign of Nero, who was imagined by many to have been revived from his suicide, and was expected to return to wreak vengeance upon the Romans and persecutions upon the Christians.

It is not until the reign of Domitian (A.D. 81–96) that the Roman emperor cult becomes highly organized and enforced throughout the empire, with the command that Christians worship Domitian as a god or suffer persecution or death. Domitian was such an infamous person that the Roman Senate refused to vote him the status of a god, so that he with his Roman legions set out to enforce worship of himself as a god, in spite of the Senate's verdict. The worst of the first-century persecutions of Christians had been brought about by Nero (A.D. 54–68) in the year 64. Historians say that he blamed the Great Fire of Rome upon the detested Christians. The terrible atrocities of Nero against the Christians were confined to Rome, and according to tradition both Paul and Peter were put to death during the times of terror. During the reign of Domitian, however, the persecution of Christians became more universal, though not so outrageous as those which took place under Nero, consisting of banishment, imprisonment, confiscation of property, and at times death.

Domitian was desirous of punishing persons who seemed politically dangerous to him, and in the case of many whom he put to death on religious charges the underlying motive was that they were dangerous in a political way. Undoubtedly towards the end of the century, with the Christians believing in a Lord whose Kingdom at his return would replace the kingdom of Rome, it was not difficult to tie political and religious reasons together as the basis of persecuting and martyring the more vehement Christians. The author of Revelation, John, was exiled by Domitian to the Isle of Patmos, a small island six by ten miles in size, off the coast of Asia Minor. It was the persecutions of Domitian which invaded the seven churches referred to in Revelation, called by Clement of Rome, a contemporary of Domitian, "the sudden and repeated calamities and adversities that have befallen us." Called the "second Nero" in Christian tradition, Domitian is the first Roman emperor who takes seriously (for Christians) the rite of being declared a god, and it is during his reign that most scholars believe Revelation was written, about A.D. 95.

"Nero Alive Again" Myth

Although the book was thus composed about a quarter of a century after the death of Nero, the person of Nero plays an important part in it. His role is related to the "Nero Alive Again" myth. In A.D. 68, when Nero was declared a public enemy by the Roman Senate for his atrocities, he escaped to a small town outside Rome and there committed suicide. Soon, however, rumors arose that he had not died, but had fled; or that he had been found by his friends, revived, and was in Parthia, the country of the dreaded barbarians who lived just beyond the eastern border of the Roman Empire; and that he was there organizing the Parthians to return under his leadership to bring revenge upon the Romans. Several impostors posed as Nero, one of them in Parthia, where he gathered a large following of Parthians, and reports of his coming caused deep fear in Asia Minor and Achaia. After a while, when Nero had not returned with his Parthian hordes, the "Nero Alive Again" myth took on greater proportions by the belief that Nero had finally died, but that he would return at some future time from the dead as the Antichrist, and would lead forces of evil against the Christians. Such a belief is implied several times in Revelation, and it is also mentioned in two other apocalyptic writings composed about the same time, the Ascension of Isaiah and the Sibylline Oracles.

While it is difficult for modern man to understand how such a wild rumor about the return of Nero could have been believed, those of us living at the close of World War II can remember the many myths about Hitler being yet alive, though his death was reported with certainty; and even to-day in 1962 there are still people who are not certain but what Hitler is still alive in some hidden resort. In Biblical history there is the expectancy that Elijah would return to herald the day of the Lord (Malachi 4 : 5); in the New Testament Jesus is thought to be a person in whom John the Baptist had returned (Mark 6 : 14ff.). In Revelation it is implied that Moses and Elijah will return as "two witnesses" (Revelation 11 : 3f.). It is thus not difficult to discern why many at the time of the writing of Revelation could believe in the "Nero Alive Again" myth. In Revelation are found several references which fit into the report that Nero had been injured, but that he would return: "the beast which was wounded by the sword and yet lived" (13 : 14); "one of its heads [that is, one of the emperors who composes the beast of ten horns and seven heads] seemed to have a mortal wound, but its mortal wound was healed, and the whole earth followed the beast with wonder" (13 : 3); "the dwellers on earth . . . will marvel to behold the beast, because it was and is not and is to come" (17 : 8).

By the time Revelation is written to the seven churches in Asia Minor, the persecutions of Domitian have become severe and extensive. The Roman soldiers at the Roman emperor cults are forcing Christians to worship the emperor or be punished, some by death; Christians without the mark indicating that they have worshipped Domitian cannot buy and sell in the marketplaces, being outlawed from a trade point of view; Jewish people in the "synagogues of Satan" are aiding the Roman soldiers in the persecutions of Christians. Some of the Christians are being true to their faith, and will not under any pressure worship Domitian as a god; but others are backsliding, abandoning the Christian faith and enjoying a release from persecution and economic deprivation, probably saying to themselves, "Is it worth all this turmoil to be a loyal Christian, when you can live a normal and prosperous life when loyal to Domitian?" Other Christians, in centers where the pressure of emperor worship is not so severe and where material prosperity exists, are becoming indifferent to the Christian cause, being content in their wealth with all the ease and luxury that it affords them. Other Christians are being over-tolerant of the various religious cults in their communities, not insisting that Christianity is the one great religion related to its Saviour Jesus Christ. Some are then simply indifferent to the Christian faith, "lukewarm, neither cold nor hot".

To the seven churches in Asia Minor—Ephesus, Smyrna, Pergamum, Thyatira, Sardis, Philadelphia, and Laodicea—John writes Revelation, imploring them to remain faithful to Christianity, not to worship Domitian, for by their faithfulness they will have their names written in the book of life, with the assurance of their reward in the New Jerusalem when the general resurrection day comes. He assures those who die as martyrs in their loyalty to Christ that their award will be a thousand-year fellowship with Christ between the first and the final resurrection day. Like the book of Daniel, Revelation has the theme: Be faithful to God and He will reward you for your faithfulness by giving you citizenship in His everlasting Kingdom. But, different from Daniel, Revelation now adds the message of loyalty to Christ, who leads faithful Christians in their battle against the evil forces of the Antichrist, embodied in the cult of Roman emperor worship.

Revelation is written to the seven churches from the Isle of Patmos by John. Patmos lay in the Aegean Sea ten miles west of Miletus and fifteen miles south-west of Ephesus, and was about sixty square miles in area. It was known as a place of banishment for upper class people who were made to labor in the quarries to pay the Roman government for the crimes they had committed. Here on this little island John was exiled for his loyalty to Christianity.

Here in his pastoral concern for the seven representative churches of Asia Minor he criticizes or encourages them in their attitudes towards the Roman emperor cult and secularism (worldliness), so that Christianity might continue with vitality. John lists the seven churches in their geographical order as a traveller moves from Ephesus north to Pergamum through Smyrna and Sardis, then south-east to Laodicea through Thyatira and Philadelphia. The problems of each of these churches were somewhat unique, but undoubtedly representative of the situations of all the churches of Asia Minor, where Christianity was fighting for its existence.

The Seven Churches

Ephesus (2: 1-7) was the most important church in Asia Minor. Paul the apostle had spent two years here lecturing in the hall of Tyrannus after speaking during three months in the synagogue. In Ephesus was a school of Christian thought, from which came the Gospel of John and the three Epistles of John. Other religious cults flourished here, such as those related to John the Baptist, Artemis (the ancient Mother Goddess of Asia Minor), gnostic cults which denied the bodily nature of Jesus, and the Roman emperor cult with its two temples. Some Christians at Ephesus, called Nicolaitans, had become lax in morality, resorting to sins of the flesh. Many of the Ephesians, originally faithful to Christ, had backslidden when the persecutions of Domitian endangered their security; some had abandoned Christian love. Ephesus as a leading church was one of the least faithful.

Smyrna (2: 8–11), the only one of the seven churches to exist to-day, was remaining spiritually alive amid economic deprivation. Christian merchants were being isolated by pagan purchasers, and Christians were finding it difficult to buy and sell in the market-places. Jews are referred to as members of the "synagogue of Satan", because they are aiding the Romans in persecuting loyal Christians. Though poor, slander-ridden, and imprisoned, the Christians at Smyrna are remaining loyal to Christ.

Pergamum (2: 12–17) was an inland city where many religious cults flourished. Some were worshipping Asklepios, whose priest wrought bodily healing for their members; a temple to Zeus attracted others; the learned and the *élite* were worshipping at the shrine of Athene, the goddess of the poets, the arts, and learning; Dionysus the Greek god of the vine had his followers; a temple for the worship of the Roman emperor had existed here since 29 B.C. Many at Pergamum are remaining faithful to Christ, but others are shifting their loyalty to the Roman emperor, while some are becoming victims of the gross sins of the flesh (referred to as followers of "the teaching of Balaam" and the Nicolaitans).

Christians in *Thyatira* (2 : 18–29) have become too tolerant of other religious cults; its members are not deeply loyal to Christian truths. Trade guilds, the Chaldean oracle of Sibyl, the shrine of Apollo (son of Zeus) are endangering the faith of Christians, who allow these cults to exist without condemning them. Gnosticism ("the deep things of Satan"), with its indifference to Jesus' bodily existence, is endangering the central theme of Christian thought, namely, the incarnation. Sexual laxity associated with the sacred prostitutes of the "Jezebel" cult (Sibyl) is undermining the morals of many people of Thyatira, allowing libertinism, or sexual freedom, to penetrate the community. Thyatira is in a bad way, and needs to come to her spiritual senses.

Sardis (3 : 1–6), formerly a wealthy capital of Lydia but now a third-rate city, has become a place of moral ease and luxurious living. Of the seven churches she has become the most degenerate. Never a city of moral idealism, she is now materially alive but spiritually dead. The dollar sign has become more prominent than the cross in the lives of the Sardis citizens; only a few have been faithful to the Christian church.

Philadelphia (3 : 7–13), in contrast to Sardis, is both wealthy and true to Christian ideals. Though the Jews ("synagogue of Satan") are co-operating with the Roman emperor cult to persecute the Christians, the people of Philadelphia are showing patient and courageous endurance, and will receive their reward when the final day of judgment arrives.

Laodicea (3 : 14–20) has become a church of indifference; she is "lukewarm"; her loyalties to Christ have been divided because her people are immersed in material prosperity and pagan religious movements. Gnostic thought, with its denial of Jesus' bodily nature, and the cult of Asklepios, with its healing allurements, are causing many Christians to backslide from loyalty to Christ. Many feel themselves "rich" in the fortunes made out of the rich woollen goods from their glossy black sheep, but they are "poor" in their spiritual living and their Christian faith.

To these seven churches John discerns Christ as offering a wonderful reward for their faithfulness, along with an admonition and a warning: "He who conquers, I will grant him to sit with me on my throne, as I myself conquered and sat down with my Father on his throne. He who has an ear, let him hear what the Spirit says to the churches" (3: 21, 22).

2. THE AUTHOR OF REVELATION

An "apocalypse" like Revelation is usually written under an assumed name, the writer borrowing the name of a well-known person in order to give the writing a note of authority. Other apocalypses have taken such authoritative names as Enoch, Moses, Solomon, Abraham, or Ezra. "John" as the author of Revelation (then as now a common name) might be the real name of the author; or the writer might be using the name of one like John the apostle, John the elder, or John Mark to bolster the prestige of his writing. Tradition has assumed John the apostle to be the author of Revelation, though the acceptance of a date of A.D. 95 for the writing of Revelation makes this rather doubtful. Since Revelation is written to the churches of Asia Minor, and an elder was presumed at this time to have authority over a number of churches, John the elder has been inferred to be the author of Revelation.

Church fathers give different "Johns'" as the writer of Revelation. Irenaeus (*Heresies*, II. 22. 5; III. 3. 4; IV. 20. 11, 30: 4; V. 26. 1) viewed John the disciple of the Lord as its author; Eusebius (*Church History*, III. 25. 2, 4; III. 39. 5–7, 14) assumed the author as John the elder; Dionysius of Alexandria (Eusebius, *Church History*, VII, 25) mentions John Mark in this regard; Justin

Martyr (*Dialogues*, 81 : 4) held the book to be by John the apostle. The lack of unity among Church fathers as to which "John" wrote Revelation leaves the modern reader equally perplexed. Though the writer behind the name "John" cannot be determined, certain characteristics of the author of Revelation stand out clearly:

(1) He is a Jew who has broad knowledge of Jewish writings, using 245 references from twenty Old Testament books. The writings he uses most are: Isaiah (54), Daniel (50), Ezekiel (31), Psalms (29), Exodus (22), Jeremiah (19), Zechariah (11), Genesis (10). Numerous references in the Old Testament relate to the plagues of Egypt. The author also quotes nine times from the New Testament (Matthew 10 : 32, 13 : 30; Mark 4 : 23, 14 : 12; Luke 21 : 24; John 1 : 1-3; Acts 2 : 20; 1 Thessalonians 5 : 2; 2 Thessalonians 3 : 18). Once he quotes from the Apocrypha (2 Maccabees 2 : 4–8).

(2) His use of Greek is not very good, which indicates that Greek was not his native language, but one that he learned later in life. (3) He appears as a person of esteemed church leadership, well acquainted with the problems of the seven churches, whose name and ideas would possess authority. (4) He is a person of deep religious convictions, whose faith perceives that God and Christ will win in the end over Satan and the demonic forces. Though the Roman emperor cult with its Roman soldiers to enforce worship of Domitian seems all-powerful in the present world, the author believes in a God and a Lord whose victorious power will reward faithful Christians by giving them citizenship in the New Jerusalem. God in the author's depth of faith can never be defeated!

(5) The author's reverence for apostles and saints, and his never mentioning personal memories regarding the life of Jesus, indicate that he was not a personal follower of Jesus. Instead he has received his knowledge of Jesus from second-hand sources. He

calls himself a "servant" of Christ (1: 1), the "brother" of his readers (1: 9), with "brother" used in a broad sense. (6) As a literary genius and a skillful user of allegory, the author has written the most artistic and influential apocalypse in Christian history. He is a skilled poetic literary artist. Most of his ideas are clothed in apocalyptic picture-language which cleverly conveys his religious message. He has left to his readers the task of fathoming the deep religious truths colored in picture and myth; but "John" believes that in these truths lies the Word of God necessary to combat the paganism of the Roman emperor cult and to bring salvation in the New Jerusalem to faithful Christians.

3. THE DATE OF REVELATION

THOUGH THE majority of scholars agree that the book of Revelation was written during the reign of Domitian (81–96) and infer the date of its composition as about 95, other dates have been suggested for its origin: (1) the latter part of the reign of Nero (54–68); (2) the reign of Vespasian (69–79), especially in the early part before the fall of the Temple in 70; (3) the reign of Claudius (41–54). The following table of dates is of value in determining the time for the writing of Revelation:

Julius Caesar	48–44 B.C.
(Roman Empire ruled by a three-man government of Antony, Octavius, and Lepidus)	
Octavius (Augustus)	27 B.C.–A.D. 14
Tiberius	14–37
Caligula	37–41
Claudius	41–54
Nero	54–68

Galba	68–69
Otho	69
Vitellius	69
Vespasian	69–79
Titus	79–81
Domitian	81–96
Nerva	96–98
Trajan	98–117

The idea that the Roman Empire is the beast depicted in Revelation, with ten horns and seven heads, has been the basis for this attempt to determine the date when the book was written. Those who favor the time of Domitian for its composition discern the ten horns and seven heads as beginning with Tiberius (14–37), since it was during his reign that Jesus' public ministry occurred. With such a basis the ten horns are: Tiberius, Caligula, Claudius, Nero, Galba, Otho, Vitellius, Vespasian, Titus, and Domitian; while the seven heads are related to the seven major emperors during this period, since Galba, Otho and Vitellius each ruled for only a few months: Tiberius, Caligula, Claudius, Nero, Vespasian, Titus, Domitian.

Epiphanius suggests the reign of Claudius as the time for the writing of Revelation, when John was on the Isle of Patmos; but such an argument seems unusual, and is not given by any other writer; and furthermore Claudius as an emperor discouraged the worship of himself by his subjects. Those who favor the reign of Vespasian as the time when the book was written begin with Julius Caesar as the first person in the beast. Thus the ten horns would be Julius Caesar, Octavius, Tiberius, Caligula, Claudius, Nero, Galba, Otho, Vitellius, and Vespasian; with the same group, minus Galba, Otho and Vitellius, indicating the seven heads. Those who doubt the time of Vespasian as the setting for the writing of Revelation do so for three reasons: (1)

his reign was not one known for its extensive persecutions; (2) the "Nero Alive Again" myth has not yet developed into the later details found in Revelation, especially regarding Nero's being chained in the underworld, from where he was expected to return; (3) there is a lack of evidence that Vespasian was forcing Christians to worship himself, even though he had his wife named Augusta, and was called Saviour and Benefactor by the citizens, with services of elaborate worship and ceremony paid to him throughout the Roman Empire.

Those who view Revelation as written in the latter days of Nero's reign base their reason upon chapters 11: 1–8, 12: 14–16, 17. There is, however, no indication among historians that Nero desired worship of himself, but rather that he persecuted Christians as scapegoats for the burning of Rome. Furthermore the "Nero Alive Again" myth would have no meaning if he were still living.

The basic reasons for holding to the year 95 in the latter part of Domitian's reign as the date when the book was written are as follows: (1) Evidence from the Church fathers: Irenaeus informs us about 180 (*Heresies*, V. 30. 3) that Revelation "was seen not long ago, but almost in our generation at the end of Domitian's reign." The Roman writer Pliny in his *Letters* (IX. 13) says that Domitian was killed on September 18 of the year 96, thus making it necessary that Revelation, if written during Domitian's reign, be written before this death date. Clement of Alexandria (Eusebius, *Church History*, III. 23) relates that "on the death of the emperor" John returned from the Isle of Patmos. (2) Domitian is the first Roman emperor to enforce worship of himself by Christians in Asia Minor. Caligula (37–41) was forcing Jews, not Christians, to worship his bust; Nero tortured the Christians, not because they did not worship him, but because he wished to punish them for the burning of Rome; emperors like Claudius and Tiberius discouraged the worship of themselves by citizens of the Roman Empire. Domitian demanded the title of "our Lord and our God," and even banished his cousin and niece for refusal to worship him. (3) The "Nero Alive Again" myth at the time of Domitian would have reached its final stages, asserting that Nero was in the underworld, soon to return to lead the forces of evil against the forces of righteousness. In its earliest stage, Nero was merely thought to have been revived after his attempted suicide and hurried to Parthia, where he was preparing to return with the Parthian hordes to wreak vengeance upon the Romans and persecute the Christians. (4) By the time of Trajan (98–117) it was considered a crime to belong to Christianity, which was considered an illegal religion. In Revelation the Christians are persecuted because they are witnesses for the Name or the Word of God (2: 13; 6: 9; 12: 11). Yet one has the feeling, in reading Revelation, that the time when Christianity would become an illegal religion is not far away.

It is safe to conclude from an analysis of the historical situation that Revelation was written about 95 by John, on the Isle of Patmos, though the final form of Revelation as we have it probably was completed at Ephesus; and that John's message was one of encouragement and condemnation during the latter years of Domitian's reign.

4. PLAN OF THE BOOK

THE BOOK of Revelation is a drama with seven acts and ten scenes, preceded by a prologue and ended with an epilogue. "Sevens" and "tens" are used in a variety of ways through Revelation, along with the author's use of numerology (the science of numbers), and the plan of the book uses them skillfully. The plan is as follows:

Prologue. 1: 1–8. A salutation is given to the seven churches in

Asia Minor, with the announcement of Christ's return. The central theme of Revelation is thus sounded. The one who speaks the message of the book through John is the Alpha and the Omega.

Act I. 1 : 9–3 : 22. *The Son of God Reigns in the Church on Earth*

Scene 1. 1 : 9–20. John in his opening vision is given his command to write.

Scene 2. 2 : 1–3 : 22. Each of the seven churches is addressed with words of warning and condemnation: Ephesus, Smyrna, Pergamum, Thyatira, Sardis, Philadelphia, Laodicea.

Act II. 4 : 1–8 : 1. *God Has a Plan for History*

Scene 3. 4 : 1–5 : 14. The court of heaven is viewed, where God is surrounded by His worshippers and His angels, with a seven-sealed scroll held in the right hand of the one seated on the throne.

Scene 4. 6 : 1–17. Each of the seven seals, indicating seven calamities, is opened: the seals represent the white horse, the red horse, the black horse, the pale horse, slain martyrs, an earthquake and the darkening of the heavenly lights [on the opening of the seventh seal, a dramatic suspense occurs with silence in heaven for half an hour, 7 : 1–8 : 1].

Act III. 8 : 2–11 : 19. *Distress Encompasses the Church*

Scene 5. 8 : 7–9 : 21. The seven trumpets, each indicating a doom, are blown: the trumpets bring forth hail and fire, an enflamed mountain thrown into the sea, a burning star falling into the abyss, one-third darkness hovering over the sun, moon, and stars; a star falling into the abyss, with smoke and locusts encompassing the earth; four angels let loose at the Euphrates [a second suspense occurs before the seventh trumpet is blown, in which is a vision of a book that is bitter and sweet, followed by a prophecy concerning Israel's repentance and the hearing of voices from heaven, 10 : 1–11 : 19].

Act IV. 12 : 1–14 : 20. *After the Battle in Heaven is Won by the Righteous, the Conflict between the Forces of Righteousness and Evil is Transferred to Earth*

Scene 6. 12: 1–14: 20. Oracles are given regarding the last judgment: the vision of the woman, the son, and the dragon (12: 1–17); the vision of the two beasts (13: 1–18); the vision of the lamb on Mount Zion (14: 1–5); warnings and promises concerning the last judgment (14: 6–20) [these form a third suspense].

Act V. 15: 1–16: 21. *The Wrath of God Descends on the World*

Scene 7. 15: 1–8. Seven bowls, each indicating a plague, visit mankind, with a partial purpose to arouse repentance in those who have been loyal to Satan: the bowls bring forth irritating sores, the sea becomes bloody, rivers and fountains become bloody, men are scorched by the sun, blasphemers are punished as the darkness descends on the kingdom, the Euphrates River is dried, lightning and thunder and earthquakes visit the earth.

Act VI. 17: 1–20: 10. *Judgment Falls on "Babylon"*

Scene 8. 17: 1–18: 24. The harlot, Babylon the Great, is destroyed, as the song of triumph is sung.

Scene 9. 19: 1–20: 10. Amid hallelujahs, Christ appears and battles Antichrist, after which the millennium occurs, the martyrs ruling with Christ and the Antichrist chained in the abyss during the 1000 year period.

Act VII. 20: 11–22: 5. *God's Final Purpose is Enshrined in the New Jerusalem*

Scene 10. 20: 11–22: 5. With the final judgment and the resurrection, the New Jerusalem as a Holy City for the righteous is portrayed.

Epilogue. 22: 6–21. After further warnings and assurances, the authority of John's revelation is testified by Jesus, followed by a final benediction.

REVELATION IS the finest example of an apocalypse in Biblical literature. The writer has been esteemed as an artist of greater ability than Bach or Coleridge or Stevenson: he has a better choice of words than Stevenson, a finer sensitivity to spiritual loveliness than Coleridge, and a better feeling for rhythm and melody than Bach. Revelation has been called "the only masterpiece of pure art in the New Testament." John is thus a *poet* whose picture-language is touched with inspiration, and as poets are never to be taken literally, John's "*poem*" of Revelation is missed if the picture-language is taken literally by the reader. Those who read Revelation must *feel* the depth of John's ideas as they unravel the religious thoughts underneath the clothing of this language. When once the modern reader *feels* John's great message of faith amidst times of persecution, then he has caught the great purpose of Revelation for his own time.

The "Science of Numbers"

Interpreters of Revelation, as in the case of Daniel, have sometimes wrongly viewed Revelation as a book to predict small details in history centuries beyond the day in which it was written. Much of their confused interpretation of Revelation's predictions has been tied to the unravelling of the number of the beast, whose number is 666. In attempting to apply a number to each of the letters of a name, thus to equal 666, odd conclusions have been brought forth in recent years as attempts to ascertain the number which John had in mind. Irenaeus (second century A.D.) interpreted 666 as LATEINOS, giving the normal numerical values to the Greek letters, and referred it to the Roman Empire. During World War II, when Hitler and Nazism seemed almost victorious over the world, another interpreter of the science of numbers viewed Hitler as the beast whose number is 666. Starting the alphabet with A=100, B=101, C=102, D=103 ... he arrived at this startling conclusion:

H I T L E R   Therefore Hitler is
107 108 119 111 104 117 =666   the beast!

Such conclusions, however, do not confirm the name which the writer of Revelation had in mind for the beast whose number is 666. They merely show what unusual things can be done with numbers and the science of numbering. John had no conception of a Hitler to come or World War II! Throughout Christian history such persons as Mohammed, Napoleon, Luther, Kaiser Wilhelm, Mussolini, Pope Benedict IX, and even the World Council of Churches have been unravelled as the beast. The beast whose number is 666 is "Nero Alive Again", and no one else. Some view 777 as a perfect number which could refer to Christ, with 666 in reference to the Antichrist, or Nero. Others have worked out 666 as referring to Nero by spelling "Nero Caesar" in Hebrew (NRWN QSR), using the numbers 50, 200, 6, 50, and 306 as applied to "Caesar" in the Hebrew, or 100, 60, 200, and 360 as related to "Nero" in the Hebrew as adding to 666, and thus applying to Nero as the Antichrist. By whatever system a person attempts to apply an unravelling of the number 666 to Nero, the conclusions of modern scholars assume that Nero is the Antichrist indicated by 666. Nero is not mentioned in Revelation by name, since in true apocalyptic fashion the number rather than the name leaves the reader with a feeling of awe and mystery; and were the name Nero, rather than the number in Revelation, read by the followers of the Antichrist, the persecutions of the Christians would have been more severely enforced.

How shall we interpret Revelation, if not as a book of prophecy to foretell present historical events? Some have felt that

Revelation as an apocalypse had meaning for first-century Christians, but that its meaning for twentieth-century persons is of little value. Martin Luther, who had little admiration for apocalypses, said that 2 Esdras, an apocalypse in the Apocrypha, was like *Aesop's Fables* and should be thrown into the River Elbe! Revelation was felt by Luther to have little value for Christians, so he placed it in an Appendix with the epistles of James, Jude, and Hebrews. But the book of Revelation is in the New Testament collection of books, and it was placed there because it spoke to the life-situations of the early Christians; and therefore it must not be *ignored* by us to-day, but *evaluated*.

Revelation should be approached by the reader through the *religious-historical* method of study. Such a way of understanding Revelation asks the reader first to place himself in the life-situation of Christians during the time of Domitian, to understand the historical situation of A.D. 95, in which Christians were being forced to worship Domitian or receive punishment; and secondly to appreciate the writer's use of myth and picture-language to clothe his religious message for his own time. After having applied this historical study of Revelation, it is then the reader's task to come back to his own time and ask what the religious message is for twentieth-century Christians. To do this he must unravel the myths and pictures for its abiding message.

Vital Set of Values

Several years ago, when the present author was writing a commentary on Revelation for laymen, he found, as he carefully got "inside" the book, a vital set of values from that volume for present-day life and thought:

(1) There is the *awfulness of sin*, especially when it is organized by political forces for compelling people to worship a temporal god, whether incarnate in a Domitian or a Hitler. Demonic

forces can grip men and corporate groups in such a way that the higher values of life are lost. The fruits of the Spirit, such as "love, joy, peace, patience, kindness, goodness, faithfulness, gentleness, self-control" (Galatians 5: 22, 23) can become smothered, and in their place sin develops the "works of the flesh" such as "immorality, impurity, licentiousness, idolatry, sorcery, enmity, strife, anger, selfishness, dissension, party spirit, envy, carousing, and the like" (Galatians 5: 19-21). Sin is an awful thing, when men become estranged from God and are gripped by demonic forces; and Revelation in a tremendous way depicts this terrifying experience.

(2) Revelation impresses upon the reader that *this is a moral universe* in which men and nations reap what they sow. There is the love of God upon His cross, but there is also the judgment of God upon His throne. Revelation puts a heavy stress upon the judgment of God, which must be discerned side by side with His redemptive love. For the moment wrong may seem victorious, but even though men die for the sake of righteousness, God as a Moral Judge brings them their reward of membership in the New Jerusalem, when the judgment day arrives; and sooner or later men receive their just deserts of reward or punishment in the present life. Revelation does note the mercy of God through the seven bowls (15: 1-8), which have a partial purpose of causing followers of Antichrist to repent. But the dominant stress in Revelation is on the moral judgment of God.

(3) Revelation is *a book meant for desperately hard times*, when persecution and death are meted to those who will not pay homage to worldly tyrants. Because of this stress, it is a book not easily understood by persons living in easy and prosperous times. But it sounds a clarion call when the going is hard: Have the courage to choose the high way; you and God are working together in an eternal venture to bring His Kingdom into the world; it is better to suffer hardships, and remain faithful to God,

than to live a life of meaningless ease through your allegiance to the evil temporal powers in the world.

(4) Christianity is a religion which has been *refined by danger and persecution*; it has been found worthy to meet the most difficult circumstances of life. Instead of singing "Faith of our fathers, living still, in spite of dungeon, fire, and sword", Revelation encourages us to sing "Faith of our fathers, living still, *because* of dungeon, fire, and sword". A faith tried and purified by the awful hardships during the time of Domitian's persecutions is worthy to meet any of life's problems and perplexities in any century.

(5) Revelation, as a person gets the larger perspective, teaches the reader that *cultures can destroy themselves*, unless they have a high religious inspiration and a deep faith in God. Had one lived at the time of Revelation as an outside observer, and made a wager as to whether the Christians would outlast the pagan citizens of the Roman Empire, he probably would have wagered against the Christians. But the year 476 arrived, and the Roman Empire went the way of great empires before her, such as Babylonia, Persia, Greece; she was destroyed, and to-day Italy is but a small country in Western Europe. But Christians to-day surround the globe with their hundreds of millions in every country on the face of the earth.

(6) Revelation is a great piece of literature, a work of literary art, the finest example of an apocalypse. While it is more than a piece of literature, since it is a deep religious writing, we to-day would be the poorer were we not the recipients of such a dramatic and beautiful specimen of apocalyptic writing as Revelation. Its influence upon art, poetry, drama, and theology has been significant.

The New Testament is a volume with more than one theological appreciation of the life, teachings, death, resurrection, and return of Jesus. Since one theological mould was not large enough to appreciate the grandeur of Jesus Christ, seven major appreciations of Jesus Christ, some of them overlapping, are found in the New Testament: those of (1) the writings of Paul; (2) the Gospel of Mark; (3) the Gospel of Matthew; (4) the Gospel of Luke, and the Book of Acts; (5) the Epistle to the Hebrews; (6) the Gospel of John, and 1, 2, 3 John; (7) Revelation. While Revelation may stand somewhat apart from the other six major interpretations of Jesus Christ in the New Testament, since it is an apocalypse, it has its unique place as a writing which has inspired millions through the Christian centuries, and still does so to-day, when apocalyptic thought with its stress on "last events in history" plays such a major part in our thought patterns. While Revelation was slow in finding a place in the canon (the final list) of New Testament writings, being especially frowned upon for a while by the Eastern Church, we to-day are fortunate that it won its place at last in the New Testament writings formally at the Council of Carthage in 397.

Guide to the Figures of Speech

Revelation as an apocalypse is so clothed with figures of speech, number-patterns, myths, and sign-language that a person, in order to understand the messages under these literary cloaks, must possess keys to unlock the spiritual treasures. The list of phrases and words with their meanings are here given to aid the reader to understand Revelation as he reads the book. Here are the "keys" arranged in alphabetical order with scripture references for the purpose of helping the reader to "open the doors" to the meaning of Revelation:

Abaddon, Apollyon (9: 11)—Abaddon is from the Hebrew, Apollyon is from the Greek, meaning a place of destruction, such as Sheol or Hades (Job 26: 6; Proverbs 15: 11).

Another (second) beast (13 : 11f.)—refers to the priests who organize the cult of Roman emperor worship, who accomplish their work by deceit and trickery, and who with the help of the Roman soldiers enforce worship of the first beast, the Roman emperor. The shape of their headdress appears like the two horns of a lamb, but this does not indicate that they are "wolves in sheep's clothing."

Alpha and Omega (1 : 8 ; 21 : 6 ; 22 : 13)—Greek words meaning "the first and the last" (1 : 17), referring to Christ as the beginning and the end; as He co-created the world with God, He will also be the co-judge with God on the resurrection day.

Babylon (14 : 8 ; 16 : 19 ; 17 : 5 ; 18 : 2, 21)—a name standing for Rome; as Babylon was the sinful city of the Babylonian Empire, Rome is now a "second Babylon" in her iniquitous practices (Jeremiah 50 : 2 ; 51 : 8 ; Isaiah 21 : 9).

Beast having ten horns and seven heads (11 : 7 ; 12 : 3 ; 13 : 1 ; 17 : 3, 7)—the cult of Roman emperor worship (the first beast) as compared with the priesthood [see *Another (second) beast*] ; its ten horns and seven heads are Tiberius, Caligula, Claudius, Nero, Galba, Otho, Vitellius, Vespasian, Titus, and Domitian as the horns; and subtracting the lesser emperors, Otho, Galba, and Vitellius, we have the seven heads, since each of these three ruled for a few months each in 68–69. It is this beast which Christians are forced to worship under Domitian.

Beast like a leopard . . . bear . . . lion (13 : 2)—the Roman emperor cult embodies all the vices and powers of the three world empires mentioned in Daniel (chapter 7) : the leopard is Babylonia, the bear is Media, the lion is Persia.

Black horse (6 : 5)—with the balance in the rider's hands, this horse stands for famine, which indicates that in the awful days ahead there will be a great scarcity of food (see Ezekiel 4 : 16f.)

Book of life (20 : 12, 15 ; 21 : 27)—here are written the names of the faithful 144,000, who will become citizens in the New Jerusalem, but which will be unknown until the resurrection day.

Bride (19: 7; 21: 2, 9; 22: 17)—as Ephesians refers to the Church as the Bride of Christ, so here the faithful followers of Christ (who compose the Church) will be "wed" to Christ as citizens in the New Jerusalem.

Darkness (6: 12; 8: 12; 16: 10; 22: 5)—in both Greek and Hebrew thought tragedy was represented by darkness; when Christ as "the Light of the world" sheds His light in the New Jerusalem, there will be no more tragedy; when the sun is but one-third darkened (8: 12), this indicates that the final and complete tragedy upon the natural world has not yet arrived. Jesus' death upon the cross, accompanied by darkness from noon to three in the afternoon (Mark 15: 33), indicates that for the moment the worst tragedy in history has occurred, based on Amos 8: 9.

Death and Hades (1: 18; 6: 8; 20: 13, 14)—Death and Hades go together, with Hades the place and Death the state of existence there; Death and Hades sometimes personify evil; Jesus as the one with the keys (1: 18), who can unlock Hades, means that He has power over Hades and Death, and can bring victory over death to faithful Christians.

Deep things of Satan (2: 24)—refers to the gnostic heresy, which denied Jesus' incarnation as a bodily person, the bodily suffering of Jesus on the cross, and the worth of the Old Testament, which they held to be the story of the imperfect creator of the natural world, called the Demiurge; the gnostics thus saw the Old Testament as the story of the imperfect creator God, while the New Testament was the story of the perfect saviour God.

Devil (2: 10; 12: 9, 12; 20: 2, 10)—Greek *diabolos*, is never used in the Old Testament, but is found thirty-two times in the New Testament; it is a Greek equivalent ("Accuser") to Hebrew *satan*, indicating the evil power in the world, which at the time of Revelation is incarnate in the Roman emperor cult.

Dragon (12: 3f.; 20: 2)—gives authority to the beast (13: 2); the dragon is the devil (12: 9), the beast is the Roman Empire.

Earthquake (8: 5; 11: 13)—the earthquake is a sign that the Day of Wrath is not far away.

Euphrates River (9: 14; 16: 12)—in Old Testament times invasion was expected to come from beyond the River Euphrates, the chief river of Babylonia and Assyria (Isaiah 7: 20; 8: 7; Jeremiah 46: 10); the river in Revelation forms the eastern boundary of the Roman Empire, over which the Parthian hordes were expected to come under the leadership of the Antichrist (Nero) and the ten Parthian generals.

First beast—see *Beast having ten horns and seven heads.*

Forty-two months (11: 2; 13: 5)—equivalent to 1260 days (11: 3; 12: 6), and "a time, and times, and half a time" (12: 14), or three and one-half years; as three and one-half years composed a time of terrible travail in the book of Daniel, when Antiochus IV dedicated the altar to the god Zeus in the Jerusalem Temple, the number now stands for the period of awful struggle which the faithful Christians during Domitian's reign must undergo before the resurrection day.

Four Living Creatures

Four living creatures (4: 6–8)—Jerome mistakenly viewed the lion in its active vigor as the Gospel of Mark, the man as the human Gospel of Matthew, the calf as an animal for sacrifice indicating the humanitarian Gospel of Luke, and the eagle, a bird of the high heavens, as the spiritual Gospel of John. The four creatures, however, as signs of the zodiac represent God's power in the world dominating all kinds of life: or, more generally, like Ezekiel's four living creatures, they are the four winds representing the powers of creation.

Gog and Magog (20: 8)—"Gog of the land of Magog" in Ezekiel (chapters 38, 39), refers to some evil leader, and here in Revelation indicates the nations deceived by the loosened Satan, who will bring havoc upon the faithful Christians before the final battle and judgment scene.

Hades (1: 18; 6: 8; 20: 13, 14)—in Revelation usually associated with *Death and Hades*; a place in the underworld, also called Sheol, where in Jewish thought all souls went after death. The Pharisees believed that all souls would arise from Hades on the resurrection day for judgment; while the Sadducees believed that all souls remained in Hades, for there was no resurrection day taught in the Law, their only scriptures. In Revelation all people at death go to Hades, awaiting the resurrection day, except the Christian martyrs, who are buried under the altar of the Temple (6: 9), an indication of the privileged burial place for those whose faith and courage faced martyrdom.

Half an hour (8: 1)—a non-literal note regarding a period of time to break with suspense the rapidly moving events in Revelation. In Revelation periods of time are always to be taken as signs rather than in a literal sense.

Hallelujah (19: 1, 3, 4, 6)—this is the only chapter in the Bible where this word of praise is used, uttered here as the woes and dirges come from the followers of the Antichrist, when the devastations of Rome begin. Hallelujah is the Hebrew for "Praise the Lord", the phrase used many times in our English translation of the Old Testament, including twenty-seven times in the Psalms.

Harlot (17: 1; 19: 2)—a term frequently applied to cities that fall away from worshipping the Lord. Isaiah (23: 17) and Nahum (3: 4) use the word in relation to Tyre and Nineveh; while Jeremiah (2: 20), Ezekiel (16: 15), and Hosea (2: 5) apply the word to Jerusalem and Israel. In Revelation it related to "Babylon," which is Rome, set on seven hills (17: 9). As a harlot through cunning ways causes men to fall for her deceitful

73

charms, so Rome with its emperor worship has used the same tactics to obtain worshippers for its cult.

Horse (6: 2, 4, 5, 8; 9: 7, 17; 19: 11, 14)—generals on an errand of peace rode an ass, but in battle they rode horses, usually a white horse. See *Black horse, Pale horse, Red horse, White horse.*

Jezebel (2: 20)—the wife of King Ahab (1 Kings 16: 31; 2 Kings 9: 22), under whose domination Baal worship with its heathen sexual practices endangered the worship of Yahweh during the time of Elijah; now related to the worship of Sibyl, which with its sacred prostitutes at her sanctuaries in Thyatira is endangering the loyalty of weak Christians. "Jezebel" may refer in Revelation to some woman who is teaching a false doctrine, and who is not necessarily a priestess of the Chaldean Sibyl cult.

King of kings (17: 14; 19: 16)—the Lamb as leader is not just another king, like the ten Parthian kings; he is the *King* of kings. The title "king", related to God in the Old Testament (Deuteronomy 10: 17; Psalm 136: 3; Daniel 2: 47; 11: 36), is now applied to Christ.

Lamb (5: 6ff.; 6: 1, 16; 7: 9ff.; 8: 1; 12: 11; 13: 8; 14: 1ff.; 17: 14; 19: 7, 9; 21: 9ff.; 22: 3)—one of the fifty-five titles related to Jesus Christ in the New Testament, used twice outside of Revelation in the Gospel of John (1: 29, 36), but found twenty-five times in Revelation. It represents the crucified saviour offered in sacrifice, who becomes the Lion (standing for the power of the resurrection).

Lion of the tribe of Judah (5: 5)—describes Christ's kingly power as the resurrected Lord, who follows the *Lamb*; the ideal king or Messiah was expected to come from the *Root of David* and the tribe of Judah (see Isaiah 9, 11); this expression is found also in Genesis (49: 9) and 2 Esdras (11: 37; 12: 31).

Little scroll (10: 2ff.)—this scroll has a vital message for the faithful Christians, telling them that terrible persecutions yet await them; thus it is bitter to eat (because of persecutions) but sweet as honey (since the awards of the New Jerusalem await them if they face the persecutions for their faith with steadfast courage). This is not to be confused with the *scroll* on which the names of the faithful are written.

Lord (4: 11; 11: 4, 15, 17; 22: 20, 21)—a title applied to God in the Old Testament, now applied to Christ, whose authority is one of *lord*ship over His faithful subjects; read Paul in Philippians 2: 5–11 for the secret of God's exalting Jesus Christ to become Lord through His humanity and His humility. See *Lord of lords*.

Lord of lords (17: 14; 19: 16)—as Lord is a title applied to many persons who have faithful subjects under them, Christ is above all earthly lords, for He as God's appointed Lord is *Lord* of lords. See *Lord*; *King of kings*.

Lord's Day (1: 10)—this expression is found in no other place in the New Testament, and refers to Sunday (the day of Christ's resurrection) as the sacred day for Christians, as contrasted to the first day of each month which was the "emperor's day". Bishop Ignatius of Antioch (about A.D. 117) speaks of the Christians: "Those who no longer 'sabbatize' but live according to the Lord's day." In 321 Constantine set aside Sunday as the Lord's Day, a time for rest and worship. The Puritans and the Westminster Confession in 1647 made the term Sabbath the same as Sunday (the Lord's Day).

Mark of the Beast

Mark of the beast (13: 16; 14: 9; 16: 2; 19: 20)—"on the right hand or the forehead" (13: 16) indicates that the mark of the beast was on the same places that the loyal Jew wore his prayer-box (phylactery). Ptolemy Philadelphus forced the sign of Dionysus to be tattooed on the hands of Jews in Alexandria

(3 Maccabees 2: 29); so it is possible that Domitian was forcing those who worshipped him to have a similar tattoo or marking; if it was absent, a person was cold-shouldered in buying and selling in the market-place, and an object of persecution. See *Seal of God* regarding the "mark" of Christians.

Michael (12: 7)—one of the seven archangels named in Enoch 20 as Uriel, Raphael, Raguel, Michael, Saraqael, Gabriel, Remiel. Michael as the champion and protector of the Jewish race (Daniel 10: 13), along with Raphael, Gabriel, and Phanuel, will now protect the Church, "the New Israel". He has power over Satan (Jude 9), and is the only archangel through whom God spoke His revelation to Moses on Mount Sinai and who knew the secret of God's creation of the world (Enoch 69: 4; Acts 7: 38).

Morning star (2: 28)—the brightest of all stars (Job 38: 7); as the morning star ushers in the light and glory of a new day, Christ as "the morning star" will bring in the glorious day for the 144,000, whose names are written in the book of life.

"Nero Alive Again" (13: 3, 12, 14; 17: 8; 19: 19)—refers to the myth about Nero's suicide in a small town near Rome, A.D. 68, when the Roman Senate had condemned him for his atrocities; the myth suggested that he was revived, taken to Parthia, and that from there he would return across the Euphrates, lead the Parthians against the Roman citizens and bring further persecutions against the Christians; later the myth developed that Nero had died and was in the underworld, whence he would return soon to lead the forces of evil against the forces of righteousness at Armageddon.

New heaven and new earth (21: 1f.)—the present world is but a copy of the perfect heaven and earth; the new heaven and new earth will be free of turmoil and sin and will be a spiritual rather than a physical place; it is the equivalent of the *New Jerusalem*.

The thought is found in Isaiah (65: 17): "For behold, I create new heavens and a new earth," and also in Isaiah 66: 22 and Enoch 91: 16.

New Jerusalem (3: 12; 21: 2, 10)—the Jewish rabbis held that there was a heavenly Jerusalem from which the earthly Jerusalem in Palestine was copied; they also taught that in heaven was a heavenly Torah (book of the law), which God revealed to Moses at Mount Sinai. John's portrait of the New Jerusalem is one which transcends earthly qualities, for it will be a cubical city like a "holy of holies", with no sea, no Temple, no tears, and no sun, moon, nor stars.

Nicolaitans (2: 6, 15)—not the followers of Nicolaus (Acts 6: 5), but a group of Christians who are engrossed in fleshly lusts, believing that salvation deals with man's soul and not with his body; they transgress the demands of the Jerusalem Council (Acts 15: 20); in the Middle Ages they were associated with the lusts of the clergy.

One hundred and forty-four thousand (7: 4—8; 14: 1, 3)—a non-literal number signifying "a great multitude which no man could number" (7: 9), whose names will be written in the book of life, and who will inherit citizenship in the New Jerusalem; "every tribe", which composes this number of persons, means the "New Israel" or the Church.

Pale horse (6: 8)—stands for plague and pestilence which accompany famine and bloodshed of war (see Ezekiel 14: 21).

Pit that is bottomless (9: 1; 11: 7; 20: 1)—usually equivalent to the gloomy abyss of Sheol or Hades, where all souls reside until the resurrection day (Romans 10: 7; Psalm 71: 20); in Revelation it is the abode where the beast is locked until the general resurrection day.

Ransom (5: 9)—an amount paid for freedom, in this instance related to the death of Jesus Christ which freed men from the tyranny of death and sin. The ransom theory of the cross was thought of by Irenaeus, Origen, Athanasius, and Augustine as coming from this view here in Revelation (and also in Acts 20: 28; 1 Corinthians 6: 20; 7: 23; 1 Peter 1: 18; and 2 Peter 2: 1), which seemed to see Christ's death as a ransom paid to the devil, by which Christ through His death (and resurrection) destroyed the power of death and the devil.

Red horse (6: 4)—standing for (1) the bloodshed and slaughter associated with the civil war in the Roman Empire, which split people into factions; and of (2) the expected torture to be brought on Roman citizens and Christians when the Parthians under Nero would invade the Roman Empire.

Root of David (5: 5; 22: 16)—the Messiah was expected to come from the line of David and the stem of Jesse (Isaiah 11: 1 10), here standing for Christ's leadership in the final Davidic Kingdom where the righteous will dwell (see also 2 Esdras 12: 32, Ecclesiasticus 47: 22).

Saints (5: 8; 8: 3, 4; 11: 18; 13: 7; 14: 12; 16: 6; 17: 6; 18: 20; 20: 9: 22: 21)—saints are mentioned twenty-seven times in the Old Testament, and sixty times in the New Testament, eleven of these instances in Revelation; a term meaning heroically devout Christians, whose faith can stand martyrdom and persecution.

Satan (2: 9, 13, 24; 3: 9; 12: 9; 20: 2, 7)—used sixteen times in the Old Testament, twelve of which are in Job, the term is employed thirty-three times in the New Testament; another word for the devil, it means the power of evil and darkness, which in Revelation is incarnate in the cult of emperor worship.

Satan's throne (2: 13)—refers to the seat of the Roman emperor cult, here at its chief center of Pergamum, but also at other places in the Roman Empire.

Scroll (5: 1ff.)—based upon a similar scene in Ezekiel (2: 9f.), the names of the faithful are written upon this scroll, but the names cannot be known until the seven seals, indicating awful calamities, have taken place. This is not to be confused with the *little scroll* (10: 2f.).

Sea was no more (21: 1)—in a maritime way of life, where many mariners were lost at sea, the sea was considered a place of evil and torment, and hence has no place in the New Jerusalem; the sea in Revelation is a lair of the beast which will devour Christians. Persian and Egyptian thought also viewed the sea as demonic.

Seal of God (7: 1f.; 9: 4; 22: 4)—as the followers of God have a mark on their foreheads or right hands, and as the pious Jew wore his prayerbox or phylactery on similar places, so the faithful Christians will wear their "mark" or have their "seal"; picture-language, it refers to the faithfulness of the Christians, who have the Spirit of the Father in their hearts (14: 1). See Ezekiel 9: 4 and *Mark of the beast*.

Second death (2: 11; 20: 6, 14; 21: 8)—all men die the first death, which is the natural death; the second death refers to the wicked sinners, who on the judgment day will not share the rewards of the resurrection; a Jewish writing speaks of "the wicked who die the second death and are assigned to Gehenna". All who do not remain faithful to the Lamb will die the second death, for they will not share the New Jerusalem or the resurrected life.

Seven bowls (16: 1ff.)—the third series of calamities, involving plagues like those in Egypt, before the faithful will receive their rewards.

Seven hills (17: 9)—Rome, which is thus called by the Roman poets Horace and Vergil, and here indicates the Roman Empire as the center of the emperor cult.

Seven seals (5: 1)—showing the first series of calamities which will occur before the names of the faithful are known in the book of life.

Seven trumpets (8: 2ff.)—the second series of catastrophes, to occur before the names of the faithful with their rewards can be known, is introduced by the blowing of the trumpets, which prepares the way for each calamity.

Sickle (14: 14f.)—the instrument for cutting grain, along with the "harvest", indicates in apocalyptic writings that the day of judgment is near.

Six hundred and sixty-six (13: 18)—a number referring to the beast that is to be worshipped, which has special references to Nero and the "Nero Alive Again" myth; see also pp. 64–5 for interpretation of this number.

Son of God (2: 18)—as Apollo, the chief deity of Thyatira, was the son of Zeus, Christ is the true Son of God; a central title of the fifty-five titles related to Jesus in the New Testament, especially in the Gospel of Mark, this is the only place where the title is used in Revelation.

Son of man (1: 13; 14: 14)—no person calls Jesus by the term "Son of man" except Stephen at the time of his martyrdom (Acts 7: 56); all other uses of the term in the four gospels have Jesus calling Himself by this title. Here the writer comes close to calling Jesus by the title, but it is "one *like* the son of man," similar to the expression in Daniel (7: 13). "Son of man" is sometimes an apocalyptic title referring to the Messiah sent from above, while at other times it means "man" or "representative man" as in the use in Ezekiel.

Synagogue of Satan (2: 9; 3: 9)—a non-literal reference to the Jews who are helping the Roman emperor cult bring persecution upon the Christians: thus their synagogue, which ought to be a place where God's love and justice are found, has in picture-language become a synagogue of Satan.

Temple of the tent of witness (15: 5f.)—as the tent in the wilderness contained the ark of the covenant, which was the agreement between God and men (Exodus 38: 21; Numbers 10: 11), so God here is making His promise to reward the faithful.

Temple not in the city (21 : 22)—there is no need of a Temple in the New Jerusalem, since the whole cubical city is a holy city; that is, the entire city is a sacred spiritual "temple" with no secular areas.

Ten kings (17 : 12f.)—these are the ten generals or satraps whom Nero will lead across the River Euphrates to bring havoc on the Christians and the citizens of the Roman Empire.

Thousand years (20 : 2f.)—a non-literal number which refers to "a long time" and which is called the millennium. *Pre-millennialism* believes that Christ will return at the beginning of this thousand-year reign on earth, a time in which the world is entirely in the hands of demonic forces; at this time the martyrs will be resurrected to reign with Christ for a thousand years, while Satan will be chained in the abyss; at the end of this thousand years the earth cleansed by fire will give to the resurrected their eternal home. *Post-millennialism* holds that the thousand-year reign of Christ will come on earth when His gospel has successfully gone to all parts of the earth; this will be followed by a horrible battle between the forces of good and evil, and then will come the new heaven and the new earth for the faithful. Neither of these theories seems to be what the writer of Revelation has in mind; he is merely indicating a long period of time yet to be endured before the final conflict.

Three and one-half days (11 : 9, 11)—indicates a time of awful calamity.

Throne (4 : 2f.; 20 : 4; 22 : 1f.)—this emphasizes God's judgment, since a judge sits upon his throne. Isaiah (6 : 1f.), Ezekiel (1 : 26–28), and Daniel (7 : 9f.) have similar scenes of God upon His throne.

Time, times, and half a time (12 : 14)—meaning a year, two years, and half a year, or three and one-half years, the equivalent of forty-two months, or 1260 days; a real time of persecution in Daniel, 168–165 B.C., but now standing for a period of persecution to be faced by faithful Christians before the resurrection day. See *Forty-two months*.

Tree of life (22: 2)—in the Garden of Eden, the perfect city of Paradise, there was but one tree of life (Genesis 2: 9), but in the New Jerusalem there are twelve trees of life, indicating the giving of eternal life to its inhabitants; the New Jerusalem will be a more abundant Paradise than the original one, before the fall of man.

Two witnesses (11: 3)—tradition said that Moses and Elijah (Mark 9: 4f.) or Elijah and Enoch would come before the arrival of the Day of the Lord on earth, but these references do not fit here in Revelation. The writer may mean by the "witnesses" the two most faithful churches, Smyrna and Philadelphia, or two Christian martyrs, who will have the qualities of Moses and Elijah, or Elijah and Enoch.

White garments (3: 18: 6: 11; 7: 9, 13)—indicating the faithful Christians who are clothed in purity.

White horse (6: 2f.; 19: 11, 13)—the beast ridden by a general in war; the white horse in 6: 2f. stands for the general who will soon invade Asia Minor to bring havoc; while the one who rides at Armageddon (19: 11) will be Christ, the victorious "general" of the righteous.

Woman clothed with the sun (12: 1f.)—this does not refer to Mary, the mother of Jesus, but to the Church, which is the "New Israel", and which "gives birth" to the Christian religion.

Wrath of God (11: 18; 14: 10; 15: 1)—Revelation, true to apocalyptic writings, places more stress on the wrath and judgment of God, than upon His mercy and forgiveness. This is due to the fact that in the time of Revelation sin has so engrossed the paganism of the world that judgment, rather than mercy and forgiveness, seems to be the primary way by which God can deal with persons who have so widely estranged themselves from

Him; they are too hardened to be touched by mercy and forgiveness.

Zion, Mountain of (14: 1)—some have thought that the writer of Revelation interprets Mount Zion to be the restored site of the earthly Jerusalem. Here, however, Mount Zion merely stands for the "heavenly Zion" or the New Jerusalem.

The Drama of Revelation Unfolded

With the introductory material before us, and the keys of interpretation at our disposal, the drama of Revelation now unfolds before us:

(1: 1–3: 21) "John", an influential Christian citizen of Asia Minor, well acquainted with the churches in that territory, was banished to the Isle of Patmos and there forced to work in the quarries, because he stood out firmly against the worship of the emperor Domitian. Being a person of deep religious convictions, accompanied by mystical, visionary experiences, he was deeply moved on a "Lord's Day" (Sunday) by God as to the events which lay ahead for both Christians and pagans. Out of this experience he gave advice, encouragement, and warning to the seven leading churches in Asia Minor. His main purpose was to instill courageous faith among his fellow-Christians in order that they would not backslide and worship at the cult of the Roman emperor, or lose themselves in the paganism of the world.

He warned *Ephesus* against the sensual living of the Nicolaitans and her abandonment of love. He encouraged *Smyrna* to continue her high faith, even though the Jews were co-operating with the supporters of the Roman emperor cult to persecute Christians. He besought the people of *Pergamum* to refrain both from the Nicolaitan practices and the worship of the emperor. He was troubled by *Thyatira* because her Christian people were too tolerant of other religious movements. *Sardis* had become self satisfied in her luxury, and had let her moral tone degenerate. *Philadelphia* was remaining faithful in a high way, as was *Smyrna*, but her members were endangered by the combined persecutions of the Jews and the members of the emperor cult. *Laodicea* was warned of her enticement by Gnosticism, her complacency, and her proud self-sufficiency.

(4: 1–8: 1) In his vision John sees a throne in heaven with one holding a scroll on which are the "144,000" who are faithful and who will receive their rewards on the judgment day. Before the judgment day arrives, worse and worse calamities will happen to Christian people. The seven seals, the seven trumpets, and the seven bowls represent terrifying events brought on by soldiers allied with the Roman emperor cult, as well as by dismaying occurrences in nature. The four horsemen are related to the first four seals and indicate victory of the Roman Empire in its warring (first seal), war and bloodshed (second seal,) famine (third seal), plague and pestilence (fourth seal). But there will be other calamities: Christians will be martyred (fifth seal); an earthquake, showing that the end is not far away, will destroy men and property (sixth seal). But the destruction will not be complete: the earth, and the sea, and the trees will not be harmed; the oil and the wine are not destroyed; only a fourth of mankind are killed. But worse calamities are ahead: this is just the beginning of tribulation! Only Christ can open the seals of the scroll: only He knows the secrets of what lies ahead. As the reader breathlessly awaits the opening of the seventh seal there is a dramatic "half-hour" of suspense.

(8: 2–11: 19) After the first suspense (silence in heaven for about half an hour) John envisions a second series of terrible events, each ushered in by a blare of a trumpet; conditions on earth are getting worse and worse. Hail and fire come to earth (first trumpet), the sea is poisoned (second trumpet), rivers and drinking water are embittered (third trumpet), darkness comes over the earth (fourth trumpet), the bottomless pit of the earth opens and brings forth locusts to destroy (fifth trumpet), plagues arrive to kill mankind (sixth trumpet). Awful as these devastations may be, they do not bring complete destruction: only a third of the waters are made bitter, bringing death to but a part of mankind; only a third of the sun, moon, and stars is darkened, indicating that the tragedy is but partial; the locusts do not harm the grass or trees, only those who have not worshipped God; the plagues kill only a third of mankind.

As the reader now anticipates the blowing of the seventh trumpet, John describes his vision of a little scroll which announces that there will be dire persecutions to follow. As the reader "digests" this awful news, it is *bitter* to swallow (persecutions are ahead), but *sweet* to taste (the resurrection day awaits those who faithfully stand persecution). As loyal Jews withstood the persecutions under Antiochus IV for three and one-half years (168–165 B.C.), so the time between now and the end of the persecutions is represented by three and one-half years, and then will come the reward of the New Jerusalem for the faithful. As the seventh trumpet is sounded the announcement is made that the kingdom of the world has become the kingdom of the Lord, but before this can occur the beast which comes from the abyss will persecute and kill many Christians, an earthquake (indicating that the end is near) will kill multitudes (7000 persons); and then God's promise from heaven will give Christians the confidence that God is with them and that the saints will be rewarded.

(12: 1–14: 20) John then has another vision; it is a battle between a woman with child (the Christian Church) and the red dragon (the Roman emperor cult). Already Michael, the protector of the Christians, has defeated Satan in heaven, and the battle is now transferred to earth, where Satan is incarnate in the

Roman emperor cult. In the battle, which will continue for "forty-two months", the second beast (the priesthood with the help of the Roman soldiers) will enforce worship of the first beast (the Roman emperor). To add horror to the terrors of the time, the return of Nero (666) is for the first time anticipated in John's vision, and will bring economic hardship to those who do not have the mark of the beast. The cutting of the harvest indicates that the end is near; the Christians are asked to keep God's commandments and the faith of Jesus a bit longer; the judgment scene is arriving. Revelation might have stopped here, but John has further things to say.

(15: 1–16: 21) Before the Israelites could reach their "promised land" and receive their deliverance from Egypt, a series of plagues broke out. In like manner John envisions another series of terrible plagues to be encountered before the faithful Christians reach their New Jerusalem on the resurrection day. The calamities are growing worse and more tormenting! John is told in his vision of the seven bowls that when these punishments have been finished, the Day of Wrath will be over; and then will come the end! [John in true literary fashion sees three times seven calamities (7 + 7 + 7) as bringing perfect and complete destruction.] As the bowls are poured there is the underlying hope that the followers of the Antichrist may be so stricken that they will repent; but they are too hardened to change their ways. Foul and evil sores come upon the followers of the Antichrist (the first bowl); the waters and the sea are poisoned, killing every living thing in the sea (second bowl); the scorching sun tortures the unfaithful (third bowl); darkness or tragedy hits the cult of emperor worship, but does not bring repentance (fourth bowl); the River Euphrates is dried, making it easy for the Parthian hordes to cross and harass the Roman citizens (fifth bowl); foul spirits like demonic frogs bring havoc on the followers of the beast (sixth bowl). The assembling for the battle at Armageddon is now in readiness; a great earthquake destroys Babylon [Rome] (seventh bowl).

The Final Visions of John

(17: 1–20: 10) The judgment of the great harlot [Rome], (which was predicted in 14: 8–16: 21) is now dramatically described in John's vision. The ten Parthian kings and their forces, led by Nero, are coming to make war against the righteous forces led by the Lamb (Christ). As Christ and His followers triumph, Rome will be brought to judgment under the wrath of God, her wealth and luxury destroyed. The faithful meanwhile will be sharing the marriage supper of the Lamb, wed to His faithful followers. In another vision John sees Christ coming on a white charger, leading His forces against those of the Antichrist. After this short battle, the Antichrist is chained in the abyss for a thousand years, while the martyrs rule with Christ a thousand years. When this period is over, Satan and his forces will surround the saints in their holy city, but fire from heaven will destroy them.

(20: 11–22: 21) In the final aspects of his visions John sees Hades giving up all the dead as the general resurrection occurs. The faithful, whose names are written in the book of life, are made citizens in the New Jerusalem, while the unfaithful are cast into the lake of fire. In the New Jerusalem there is no more suffering and sorrow; there is no need of a temple, because the whole city is a cubic "holy of holies", or temple; in the holy city there is no sea; the city has neither day nor night, since it is a spiritual place with God radiating light to its citizens; in it are twelve trees of eternal life for all to enjoy. The wedding is now complete, as the Lamb (Christ) is married to the Bride (His faithful followers).

As the drama ends John assures his readers that his visions are complete, and that all of this will soon take place; for Christ says,

"Surely I am coming soon." A message meant for the days immediately following A.D. 95, its poetic song of faith and encouragement in hard times has meant much to millions throughout the Christian centuries, and continues to have an abiding message for us to-day.

POWER OF THE BOOKS

SOME PERMANENT VALUES IN REVELATION AND DANIEL

It has been wisely said that "the lesson of life is to learn what the centuries have to say to the hours". Certainly this axiom is true when a person reads the great portions of the Bible, and particularly from Daniel and Revelation. Though these two books were written in the setting of the Near East in a handicraft-pastoral era many centuries ago, they have much to say to us in the twentieth century, living in an industrial setting in a scientific age of the Western world; they contain timeless truths, which penetrate into modern life.

(1) Religion to-day is deeply concerned with the last events in history. Albert Schweitzer in his first book written in 1903, entitled *The Mystery of the Kingdom of God*, aroused us to the study of the New Testament in an apocalyptic atmosphere. To be sure, not all Christian thinkers agree upon the type of study of the last things which fits our age best, and not all New Testament books see the last things in exactly the same light. This was clear at the Assembly of the World Council of Churches in Evanston, Illinois in 1954, when two papers on "the last events" were read, one by a professor of theology from Heidelberg University (Germany) and the other by a professor of theology from Yale University (United States of America). That from Europe was pessimistic about the present world, while that from America was hopeful about the world in which we live. But the main point is, that the last events, the end of history, was the central theme of this great series of meetings. A reading of Daniel and Revelation

with helpful commentaries aids one greatly in refining one's views upon this theme, at a time when a basic question in all our hearts is, "What lies ahead for our civilization?" In times of wars and "cold wars" this question cannot be avoided by any thoughtful person.

(2) No books go more deeply into the resurrection life than do Daniel and Revelation. The Law books of the Old Testament said nothing about life beyond the grave; and the Hebrew prophets focused their main attention upon the present world. Ezekiel and Hosea did hold views about a national resurrection day, but their attitude towards the resurrection related only to righteous Israelites. Daniel is the only Old Testament writing which deals with everlasting life, and which views a resurrection of both the righteous and the wicked, though the theme is dealt with in Enoch, 4 Maccabees, and the Psalms of Solomon. Whereas Daniel seems to imply that only the saints will share the resurrection day and that the worst sinners have everlasting punishment, Revelation views the resurrection day as concerned with all humanity, with rewards of everlasting life for the righteous and the "second death" for the unrighteous. At a time when many think of everlasting life merely in terms of social influence upon a community or biological immortality through one's heredity, it is necessary to read books like Daniel and Revelation which point one's thoughts to the continuity of the individual self beyond the grave, and to have an assurance that God, who conserves values, is concerned that individual persons of spiritual worth never perish.

Church and State

(3) Both Daniel and Revelation look at the problem of the relationship between the church and the state with a needed focus, at a period in history where this is a penetrating problem. Jesus

faced the problem, when He replied, "Render to Caesar the things that are Caesar's, and to God the things that are God's" (Mark 12: 17). Paul said, "Let every person be subject to the governing authorities. For there is no authority except God, and those that exist have been instituted by God . . . Pay taxes, for the authorities are ministers of God" (Romans 13: 1, 6). 1 Peter says, "Fear God. Honor the emperor" (2: 17). The New Testament sees the state with its function and the church with its province of authority; the church and the state are not contrary in purpose and should work together. But when the state takes over the function and authority of the church (or the temple), as in the instances of Daniel and Revelation, and where the state creates its own gods to be worshipped, then religion rebels. Daniel and Revelation are saying with vehemence: When the state creates its gods to be worshipped, and thus goes beyond its proper duties, loyal religionists must speak out, and remain loyal in worship to their only true God. Many people in our generation were loyal to the German state and to the church or the synagog; but when they were forced to "heil" Hitler, they went the way of martyrs, since the German state had usurped the authority of organized religions. Books like Daniel and Revelation interpret the convictions of loyal religionists, when the state takes over the province of religion.

(4) Political life of any culture is unsafe, if it degenerates religiously and morally. It is suggested that a saint should be near every great political leader to give him advice during the stress and strain of his labors. Daniel and Revelation help us to clarify this point to-day as we try to grasp a philosophy of history. Babylonia, Media and Persia, Greece, and Rome had their heydays of glory and world domination; but in due time each of these great empires fell, largely because their cultures went to pieces morally and religiously. A historian tells us that a basic reason for the fall of the Roman Empire in 476 was due to the

fact that her Roman soldiers no longer felt confidence in an ideal worth fighting for and conserving. To-day as Western culture, which is based upon the concept of a Christian democracy, is vying with the godless materialism of Communism, men are asking, "Which ideology is going to win?" Revelation and Daniel urge us to keep God at the center of our culture, for to the degree that we do this can we be assured of victory. Woodrow Wilson not many weeks before his death said to a friend of his, as they were talking about world peace and the League of Nations, "Nothing can stop God!" Revelation and Daniel ask us to keep such a thought central.

(5) There are people to-day who are sure that the laws of nature cannot be broken, but who have an indifference to the sureness of the moral laws of the universe. Daniel and Revelation are saying to such individuals, "You can no more break the moral laws of the universe than you can the natural laws, and get away with such an act. If you jump from a ten story building and are killed, you are merely illustrating the natural law of gravitation; you are not breaking it. The same is true of the moral laws of the universe; you can illustrate them, but you cannot break them. You reap what you sow." Daniel and Revelation view the universe as a three story structure: the heaven above, the earth, and Hades below; while we to-day view our universe as an organic whole, a *universe*. Though we have a different portrait of the universe to-day from that held by Daniel and Revelation, the same God is in control and the moral laws are still just as constant as are the laws of nature. Both Daniel and Revelation are saying that if just rewards to the righteous do not come this side of the grave, the rewards do come for all as they share the resurrection life beyond the grave in God's eternal Kingdom, or in the New Jerusalem.

(6) Daniel and Revelation laud religion with its rites, its prayers, its laws, its organization as absolutely necessary in the

temple or the church. We need both the prophets and the priests in religion. The prophets sound their call for social justice, and keep the moral tone of religion in a state of growth; they keep religion from becoming a curiosity. But the priests are also needed to give unity and organized strength to people who belong to a religious faith. They stress this unity through a Bible, hymns, creed, ritual, officers, organized group-life. If Judaism and Christianity had not had the temple and the church, around which its devotees found allegiance through its forms and organizations, Judaism could not have combatted Antiochus IV and Greek religion, and Christianity would have been no match against the Roman emperor cult during the time of Domitian. How fortunate our generation is to have such an organization as the World Council of Churches, trying to unify the world through its principles, when our world at various times has organized its secular forces around the tools of war.

Christ is Victor

(7) Daniel and Revelation view God as the King of kings. Both books are asking that we never lose our loyalty to God. Neither book tells its devotees that loyalty to God will necessarily bring momentary ease and prosperity: banishment, confiscation of property, economic loss, and even death may be one's reward for loyalty to God. This loyalty to God also asks that faithful persons organize to fight evil and sin, and bids them not to adjust themselves to organized evil in the world. Both books say, however, that the Cross and the Crown go together. God does reward those who remain faithful to Him. He invites His followers to live each day for all that it is worth, dauntless and unafraid, leaving the future in His hands. As He has watched over His faithful followers in the past, He will do so to-day, and in the

future. *Trust God and be not afraid* is the clarion call of faith in Daniel and Revelation.

(8) Revelation sounds forth Christ and its primary note is: *Christ is Victor*! The New Testament has fifty-five rich titles applied to Jesus Christ. Of these Revelation speaks of Christ as Son of God (once), one like unto the son of man (twice), the Alpha and the Omega (three times), the Lamb (twenty-five times) who becomes the Lion, Lord (six times), Lord of lords (twice), King of kings (twice). Never before had the titles of Lord of lords or King of kings been assigned by Jews or Christians to anyone but God. Now Christ as Victor has these titles designated for His power and His authority. Revelation links the centrality of Christ with the centrality of God in such a way that their powers seem alike. Christ is Victor, because the One who reveals Himself through Christ is the God of the universe, who will never be defeated, and who will remain victorious with His faithful followers for ever and for ever!